Water During and After Armed Conflicts

Water During and After Armed Conflicts

What Protection in International Law?

By

Mara Tignino

BRILL

LEIDEN | BOSTON

Library of Congress Control Number: 2016955570

Typeface for the Latin, Greek, and Cyrillic scripts: "Brill". See and download: brill.com/brill-typeface.

ISBN 978-90-04-33841-8 (paperback)
ISBN 978-90-04-33842-5 (e-book)

Originally published as Volume 1(4) 2016, in *International Water Law*, DOI 10.1163/23529369-12340004.

This book is printed on acid-free paper and produced in a sustainable manner.

Contents

BRILL

INTERNATIONAL WATER LAW 1.4 (2016) 1–111

BRP
brill.com/brp

Water During and After Armed Conflicts

What Protection in International Law?

Dr Mara Tignino
Senior Lecturer and Coordinator of the Platform for International Water Law/ Geneva Water Hub, Faculty of Law, University of Geneva Bd. Carl-Vogt, 66 1205 Geneva
mara.tignino@unige.ch

Abstract

Armed conflicts damage water installations and limit access to the resource. It was only in the 1970s, however, that international humanitarian law (IHL) established norms to limit the impact of armed conflicts on water resources. This monograph contends that the protection provided by IHL norms should be expanded to take into account the wide range of existing principles and rules relating to water enshrined in human rights law and international water law. Although these rules are designed for distinct purposes, ranging from regulation of hostilities and the uses, management and protection of water, they are not distinct legal regimes to be interpreted and applied independently. Accordingly, the monograph argues and concludes that protection of water resources in times of armed conflict must be assessed against an extensive and holistic set of principles and rules of international law.

Keywords

Armed conflict – post-conflict – human right to water – environment

Introduction

The relation between fresh water and armed conflicts may be seen from many perspectives and different angles: water may be the object of cooperation between states or be one of the factors triggering armed conflicts. The purpose of this monograph is to assess the role of international law in the protection of

 | DOI 10.1163/23529369-12340004

water during and after armed conflicts. The protection of water resources and water-related installations in armed conflicts has been viewed primarily through the lens of international humanitarian law (IHL). This perspective, however, is overly narrow and should be broadened to include other areas of international law, such as human rights law and international water law.

As research since the 1990s has shown, water may be a, but never the sole, factor leading to an armed conflict. A prime example of such a relationship between armed conflict and natural resource disputes is the Darfur conflict, characterized by rivalry between local communities and tribes for access to arable land and water resources.[1] Inequality in the distribution of natural resources and risks of shortage are contributing causes of tension and conflict between states. Most scholars agree that 'water wars' are myths.[2] Indeed, the number of international agreements about water bear witness to the willingness of states to peacefully settle conflicts over the use of fresh water resources.[3]

Water is a weapon and a strategy of war, but also a vulnerable resource in need of protection.[4] The strategic and military value of water has long been recognized. In 1994, an International Committee of the Red Cross ('ICRC') Expert Meeting affirmed that, during an armed conflict, lack of access to safe water and public health problems may kill as many people as bombs.[5] Twenty-one years later, in 2015, an ICRC study found that fifty million people living

1 United Nations Environment Programme, Sudan: Post-Conflict Environmental Assessment, 2007. Available at: http://www.unep.org/sudan/post-conflict/PDF/UNEP_Sudan.pdf.

2 T. Homer-Dixon, 'The myth of global waters war', *in*, *Forum: Water and War* (Geneva: International Committee of the Red Cross, 1998), p. 11.

3 A. Woolf, 'Conflict and Cooperation Along International Waterways', *Water Policy*, Vol. 1(2) (1998), pp. 251–265.

4 A few studies are devoted to the protection of water during armed conflicts, see Mara Tignino, *L'eau et la guerre: éléments pour un régime juridique*, Geneva Academy of International Humanitarian Law and Human Rights Law, (Bruylant, 2011); Theo Boutruche, 'Le statut de l'eau en droit international humanitaire', *International Review of the Red Cross*, Vol. 82 (840) (2000), pp. 887–916, https://www.icrc.org/fre/resources/documents/misc/5fzhpx.htm, last accessed on 16 January 2016; Ameur Zemmali, 'La protection de l'eau en période de conflit armé', *International Review of the Red Cross*, Vol. 77 (815) (1995), pp. 601–615, https://www.icrc.org/fre/resources/documents/misc/5fzg2p.htm, last accessed on 15 October 2016; Wilfried Remans, 'Water and War', *Humantäres Völkerrecht*, Vol. 8(1) (1995), pp. 1–14; Philipp Stucki, 'Water Wars or Water Peace? Rethinking the Nexus between Water Scarcity and Armed Conflict', Occasional Paper No. 3, *Programme for Strategic and International Security Studies*, Graduate Institute of International and Development Studies (2005); N. Jorgensen, 'The Protection of Freshwater in Armed Conflict', *Journal of International Law and International Relations*, Vol. 3(2) (2007), pp. 57–96.

5 Homer-Dixon, supra, note 2, p. 10.

in urban areas are affected by armed conflicts and suffer from restricted water supplies.[6]

Analysis of past and recent armed conflicts shows that attacks on water infrastructures are integral to military strategy. During the Korean War, U.S. air strikes damaged the dams that provided irrigation water to the north of the country, and during the Vietnam conflict dams and dykes were also seriously damaged.[7] In recent decades, belligerents have taken control of dams and dykes to strengthen their hold over occupied territories. Dams in the Tigris and Euphrates Rivers controlled by the Islamic State in Iraq and Syria are cases in point.[8] Moreover, power plants may also be a target of military operations. These facilities may have a dual function and be used for pumping water to civilian populations but also for supporting military activities.[9] Although IHL contains rules to protect these facilities, these norms should be reinforced to ensure adequate protection of water and energy installations.

The protection of water resources and installations is partly achieved by IHL, whose object is to regulate armed conflicts and particularly the conduct of hostilities. Some of its instruments, primarily the First Additional Protocol to the Geneva Conventions relating to the protection of victims of international armed conflicts ('First Protocol') and the Second Additional Protocol to the Geneva Conventions relating to the protection of victims of international armed conflicts ('Second Protocol') include a series of norms aimed at directly protecting water, such as those regarding the prohibition on attacking and destroying objects indispensable to the survival of the civilian population

6 Jean Philippe Dross; Michael Talhami; Evaristo de Pinho Oliveira; Javier Cordoba & Mark Zeitoun, *Urban Services During Protracted Armed Conflicts* (Geneva: International Committee of the Red Cross, 2015), https://www.icrc.org/eng/assets/files/publications/icrc-002-4249.pdf, last accessed on 15 October 2016.

7 Yves Sandoz; Christophe Swinarski & Bruno Zimmerman, *Commentary on the Additional Protocols of 8 June 1977 to the Geneva Conventions of 12 August 1949* (ICRC/Martinus Nijhoff, 1987), p. 685.

8 Tobias von Lossow, 'Water as Weapon: IS on the Euphrates and Tigris. The Systematic Instrumentalisation of Water Entails Conflicting IS Objectives', *German Institute for International and Security Studies* (2016), https://www.swp-berlin.org/fileadmin/contents/products/comments/2016C03_lsw.pdf, last accessed on 15 October 2016.

9 For example, during the conflict in Kosovo, air strikes on a power plant in Bor and the consequent reduction of electricity interrupted the production of sulphuric acid, a product of the copper industry. United Nations Environment Programme and United Nations Centre for Human Settlements (Habitat), *The Kosovo Conflict: Consequences for the Environment and Human Settlements* (1999), p. 49, available at: http://www.grid.unep.ch/btf/final/finalreport.pdf. See infra for the analysis of 'dual use' objects.

and the prohibition on attacking works and installations containing dangerous forces, such as dams and dykes. Another set of norms relates to protecting the environment from the effects of war. While these norms represent definite progress, they remain deficient. For instance, they only protect access to natural resources like water in extreme cases of need or pollution.[10]

The monograph will analyse the various principles and rules of IHL devoted to the protection of water and discuss how international criminal law could strengthen the protection of water during armed conflicts (Section A). Secondly, the monograph will look at the regimes for protection of water under international water law and environmental law (Section B). These areas of international law, in particular, have paid attention to the protection of water in conditions of armed conflict. In this context, the monograph will focus on the regimes of specific watercourses, such as the Danube River, as such regimes provide valuable insights into the points of contact and interaction between IHL and international water law. The monograph will then examine the relationship between human rights law and access to water. For example, human rights investigatory mechanisms will be examined to assess their contribution to the development of the rules applicable to water resources in armed conflicts (Section C). The last section of the monograph will address post-conflict and peace-building. These processes broach issues related to environmental assistance, the obligations of clean-up, the 'responsibility to protect' the population from deliberate limitation to water supplies essential to survival, and the importance of access to legal mechanisms for individuals and communities affected by armed conflicts (Section D). The analysis of this complex mosaic of corps of norms, including IHL, human rights law and international water law during and after armed conflicts, points to the potential benefits of having a single legal instrument dealing with water and armed conflicts.

A The Protection of Water under International Humanitarian Law

Unlike peacetime legislation, IHL contains few rules that relate directly to the protection of fresh water resources. Nevertheless, access to and protection of water may well become problematic during and after armed conflicts. IHL did not provide norms aimed at limiting the impact of armed conflicts on water and the environment until the 1970s. Some of these rules deal directly with the protection of water and the environment. In this respect, this monograph analyses the provisions of the 1977 First and Second Protocols, which prohibit

10 Tignino (2011), supra, note 4.

attacks against water installations. Articles 54 and 56 of the First Protocol and Articles 14 and 15 of the Second Protocol prohibit attacks against objects indispensable to the survival of the population and against dams and dykes. Attacking such structures has harmful effects on both the population and the environment (Part I).

The monograph also considers IHL provisions that protect water indirectly. In this respect, I will examine the provisions of the First Protocol, which prohibit 'widespread', 'long-lasting' and 'serious' damage to the environment.[11] The monograph will compare these to the damage, which is different in scope but described in similar terms, contemplated by the Convention on the prohibition of military or any hostile use of environmental modification techniques ('ENMOD Convention'), which was adopted one year earlier than the two Protocols, in 1976 (Part II). The relationship between these norms and the protection of water must be reinforced to ensure that environmental protection is effectively implemented during armed conflicts. In the context of IHL, I will also discuss the role that is played by general principles, such as the principle of proportionality, the principle of distinction and the prohibition of indiscriminate attacks (Part III). Finally, I will examine whether the protection of the environment under international humanitarian law can be strengthened by an appeal to international criminal law. To this end, I will analyse certain provisions of the Rome Statute of the International Criminal Court ('ICC') and the relevant practice of the ICC, particularly the warrant issued for the arrest of President Omar Al Bashir (Part IV).[12]

I *The Protection of Access to Water*

In recent decades, demand for water has increased significantly. Moreover, there has been increased recognition that protecting water resources and water installations is vital for the health and survival of people all over the world.

11 Article 35.3, titled 'Basic rules', provides that: "It is prohibited to employ methods or means of warfare which are intended, or may be expected, to cause widespread, long-term and severe damage to the natural environment." For its part, Article 55, titled 'Protection of the natural environment', provides that: "1. Care shall be taken in warfare to protect the natural environment against widespread, long-term and severe damage. This protection includes a prohibition of the use of methods or means of warfare which are intended or may be expected to cause such damage to the natural environment and thereby to prejudice the health or survival of the population. 2. Attacks against the natural environment by way of reprisals are prohibited."

12 *Decision on the Prosecution's Application for a Warrant of Arrest against Omar Hassan Ahmad Al Bashir*, International Criminal Court, Pre-Trial Chamber (4 March 2009), para. 91, http://www.icc-cpi.int/iccdocs/doc/doc639096.pdf, last accessed on 20 January 2016.

At the same time, the destructive power of weapons has greatly increased, so that water installations remain particularly vulnerable and highly susceptible to damage and destruction.

The protection of water resources under IHL includes the prohibition against attacking drinking water supplies, irrigation works (Part 1), and dams and dykes (Part 2). I will examine these prohibitions in the following sections.

1 The Protection of Objects Indispensable to the Survival of the Civilian Population

The first paragraph of Article 54 of the First Protocol states, as a general principle, that "starvation of civilians as a method of warfare is prohibited." The second paragraph develops the general principle in terms of practical modalities:

> It is prohibited to attack, destroy, remove or render useless objects indispensable to the survival of the civilian population, such as […] drinking water installations and supplies and irrigation works, for the specific purpose of denying them for their sustenance value to the civilian population or to the adverse Party, whatever the motive, whether in order to starve out civilians, to cause them to move away, or for any other motive.[13]

Drinking water supplies, such as water installations and irrigation works, are of course expressly protected by this rule.[14] The Commentary of the International Committee of the Red Cross on the Additional Protocols ('ICRC Commentary') affirms that "the verbs 'attack', 'destroy', 'remove' and 'render useless' are used to cover all possibilities, including pollution by chemical or other agents of water reservoirs."[15] This protective rule is strengthened by the fourth paragraph of Article 54, which forbids reprisals on such objects.

Despite this, paragraph 3 of Article 54 establishes that the immunity of indispensable objects is lifted where they serve as sustenance solely for members of the armed forces or as direct support for military action.[16] This exception

13 Article 54.2 of the First Protocol.

14 The same wording is used in Article 14 of the Second Protocol which cites "drinking water installations and supplies and irrigation works" as indispensable objects.

15 Sandoz; Swinarski & Zimmerman, supra, note 7, p. 655.

16 Article 54.3 states that: "The prohibitions in paragraph 2 shall not apply to such of the objects covered by it as are used by an adverse Party: (a) as sustenance solely for the members of its armed forces; or (b) if not as sustenance, then in direct support of military action, provided, however, that in no event shall actions against these objects be taken which may be expected to leave the civilian population with such inadequate food or water as to cause its starvation or force its movement."

constitutes a gap in the protection of water during international armed conflicts. It is unlikely, however, that any water installations would be used solely for the benefit of armed forces or that drinking water supplies could be used in direct support of military action.[17] Although some water supplies could serve to sustain the armed forces, this possibility is not a sufficient reason to deprive water of the level of protection guaranteed by the treaty. This view is confirmed by the restriction contained at the end of paragraph 3, which states that belligerents must nevertheless refrain from acts which may be expected to reduce the civilian population to starvation or force them to move away.

The last paragraph of Article 54 is related to the use of scorched earth warfare.[18] This military strategy has devastating effects on the civilian population and was used by the German state during the Second World War. Article 54.5 establishes that a belligerent power may in an extreme case destroy objects indispensable to the survival of the civilian population in that part of its own territory that is under its control. However, an occupying power is prohibited from destroying such objects when they are located in occupied territories.[19] The scorched earth tactic is forbidden in occupied territories and the objects indispensable to the survival of the civilian population must therefore not be destroyed.

There are significant examples—from the 2006 Lebanon war and the 2011 intervention by the North Atlantic Treaty Organization ('NATO') in Libya to the conflict in Syria—where the targeting of water supplies, sanitation systems and electrical facilities caused serious disruption and deprived the population of water supplies.[20] It can be difficult, however, to apply Article 54 to these incidents if the purpose of the military actions was not to deprive the civilian population of essential water supplies.

It is interesting to note that, upon ratification of the First Protocol, France and the United Kingdom stated that Article 54.2 did not apply to attacks that were carried out for a specific purpose other than denying sustenance to the civilian population.[21] These reservations have been questioned as they serve

17 Sandoz; Swinarski & Zimmerman, supra, note 7, pp. 656–657.

18 Article 54.5 provides that: "In recognition of the vital requirements of any Party to the conflict in the defence of its national territory against invasion, derogation from the prohibitions contained in paragraph 2 may be made by a Party to the conflict within such territory under its own control where required by imperative military necessity."

19 Sandoz; Swinarski & Zimmerman, supra, note 7, p. 659.

20 Peter H. Gleick, 'Water, Drought, Climate Change, and Conflict in Syria', *Weather, Climate and Society*, Vol. 6(3) (2014), pp. 331–339, at p. 336.

21 The reservation of the United Kingdom reads as follows: "The United Kingdom understands that paragraph 2 has no application to attacks that are carried out for a specific

only to underscore the specific scope of Article 54.[22] As described in further detail in Case Study 1, the tribunal established under the auspices of the Permanent Court of Arbitration ('PCA') rejected the relevance of the British and French reservations with regard to the application of Article 54 during the conflict between Ethiopia and Eritrea.

> The protection of water reservoirs under international humanitarian law has been analysed by the Eritrea-Ethiopia Claims Commission, established under the auspices of the PCA. In 1999 and 2000, Ethiopia attacked the Harsile water reservoir located near the port city of Assab in Eritrea. This reservoir provided the city with its only source of drinking water. The Commission examined the application of Article 54 to these attacks, pointing out that "none of the 160 States that have become Parties to the Protocol has made any reservation or statement of interpretation rejecting or limiting the binding nature" of the prohibition against attacking objects indispensable to the survival of the civilian population. The Commission indicated that only two reservations made by the United Kingdom (UK) and France purport to limit the scope of this prohibition. But, according to the Commission, the UK statement "merely emphasizes what paragraph 2 of Article 54 says, i.e. that it prohibits only attacks that have the specific purpose of denying sustenance to the civilian population or the adverse Party". For its part, the statement by France aims at preserving "a right to attack objects used solely for the sustenance of members of the armed forces". The Commission concluded that Article 54 has a customary character and found that Ethiopia had violated the prohibition on depriving the population of an object indispensable to its survival. According to the Commission, this prohibition "has been very widely accepted" and "has become part of customary international humanitarian law."[23]

Case Study 1: Eritrea-Ethiopia Claims Commission.

---

purpose other than denying sustenance to the civilian population or the adverse party." (2 July 2002), https://www.icrc.org/ihl.nsf/NORM/0A9E03F0F2EE757CC1256402003FB6D2?OpenDocument, last accessed on 21 February 2016.

22 Michael Bothe; Karl J. Partsch & Waldemar A. Solf, *New Rules for Victims of Armed Conflicts: Commentary on the Two Protocols Additional to the Geneva Conventions of 1949* (Martinus Nijhoff Publishers, 1982), p. 330.

23 PCA, *Eritrea-Ethiopia Claims Commission—Partial Award: Western Front, Aerial Bombardment and Related Claims—Eritrea's Claims 1, 3, 5, 9–13, 14, 21, 25 & 26*, Decision of 19 December 2005, *Reports of International Arbitral Awards*, Vol. XXVI, pp. 329–330, para. 105.

The adoption of the ICC Statute strengthens the rules contained in Article 54 of the First Protocol. Under the ICC Statute, "intentionally using starvation of civilians as a method of warfare by depriving them of objects indispensable to their survival" is a war crime in international armed conflicts.[24] The Preparatory Commission for the ICC supports a broad understanding of the notion of 'starvation', affirming that

> In accordance with major dictionaries, it [starvation] was meant to cover not only the more restrictive meaning of starving as killing by deprivation of water and food, but also the more general meaning of deprivation or insufficient supply of some essential commodity, of something necessary to survival.[25]

In non-international armed conflicts, the prohibition on starvation is mandated by Article 14 of the Second Protocol.[26] The prohibition on attacking objects indispensable to the survival of the civilian population is also set forth in this Protocol and is defined as a corollary to the prohibition on starvation. Unlike international conflict situations, there is no exception to this prohibition. This rule is of particular importance since the Second Protocol does not include a general protection of civilian objects. The Protocol does not distinguish between objects intended for the armed forces and those intended for civilians. Article 14 would be meaningless if one could invoke the argument that members of the government's armed forces or the armed opposition might make use of the objects in question. This prohibition falls under the responsibility of the warring parties to guarantee humane treatment for all persons not participating in hostilities and prohibits violence to life in particular. Although the ICC Statute does not list starvation as a war crime during a non-international armed conflict, it does list the pillage and the destruction of property. Both crimes may cover attacks against drinking water supplies.

24 Article 8.2 (b) (xxv) of the ICC Statute.

25 Knut Dörmann, 'Preparatory Commission for the International Criminal Court: the Elements of War Crimes', *International Review of the Red Cross*, Vol. 83 (842) (2001), pp. 461–487, at p. 475 (footnote omitted).

26 Article 14 reads as follows: "Starvation of civilians as a method of combat is prohibited. It is therefore prohibited to attack, destroy, remove or render useless, for that purpose, objects indispensable to the survival of the civilian population, such as foodstuffs, agricultural areas for the production of foodstuffs, crops, livestock, drinking water installations and supplies and irrigation works."

2 The Prohibition on Attacking Works and Installations Containing Dangerous Forces

During armed conflicts, dams and dykes often represent a tempting target for warring parties. In the last few years, efforts to control strategic dams on the Tigris and Euphrates Rivers have been at the centre of military operations carried out by the Islamic State ('IS') in Syria and Iraq, as elaborated further in Case Study 2.

> The takeover of the Mosul dam in 2014 by the Islamic State (IS) set off alarm bells around the world. The IS's control over water installations allows it to draw on large amounts of water and energy to sustain the extraction, processing and sale of crude oil that provide funding for the militia. The US-led anti-IS coalition supported both the Kurdish and Iraqi armies in their efforts to maintain or regain control over the Euphrates and Tigris river dams, with the aim of impeding the takeover of strategic installations that strengthen the powers of the caliphate in the Middle East. Some dams like Tabqa in Syria, remain in the hands of the IS.[27]

Case Study 2: Control of Dams in the Tigris and Euphrates Rivers.

The hostile control of dams gives rise to three types of risk. The first type of risk is that too little water will be available to the civilian population. Whoever controls the dams can cause downstream droughts and cut off energy and water supplies for entire towns. The second type of risk is the release of too much water, flooding kilometres of farmland, killing livestock and causing casualties and displacement. A third type of risk involves the quality of the water. It has been reported that the IS poisoned drinking water supplies in Aleppo and Baghdad. Moreover, in 2015, a threat to poison water supplies in Pristina was prevented just before it was carried out.[28]

The prohibition on attacking such installations responds to the concern that the partial or complete destruction of dams and dykes would have catastrophic impacts on the population. Moreover, the protection of these objects ensures access to drinking water. These installations often provide the hydroelectric energy that is indispensable to providing drinking water supplies. During the Diplomatic Conference on the Reaffirmation and Development of International Humanitarian Law Applicable in Armed Conflicts of 1974–1977,

27 Von Lossow, supra, note 8.

28 Von Lossow, supra, note 8, p. 3.

several state representatives underlined the importance of ensuring a strong framework of protection for hydroelectric installations. The representative of Vietnam, in particular, affirmed that the bombing of dams in North Vietnam, which was systematically carried out by explosive and perforating bombs, may have been comparable in its effects to a hydrogen bomb: the flooding of the Red River Delta, the destruction of rice plantations, and the death of two or three million people caused by flooding and starvation.[29]

In light of the extremely serious effects that damage to water infrastructure can have on the life and property of the civilian population, Article 56 of the First Protocol[30] and Article 15 of the Second Protocol[31] forbid any damage to dams that may have an impact on the civilian population. Article 56 also provides that even military targets located at or in the vicinity of particular

29 'Official Records of the Diplomatic Conference on the Reaffirmation and Development of International Humanitarian Law Applicable in Armed Conflicts', *International Committee of the Red Cross*, Vol. XIV, CCDD/III/SR.19 (1977), p. 161.

30 Article 56 affirms that: "1. Works or installations containing dangerous forces, namely dams, dykes and nuclear electrical generating stations, shall not be made the object of attack, even where these objects are military objectives, if such attack may cause the release of dangerous forces and consequent severe losses among the civilian population. Other military objectives located at or in the vicinity of these works or installations shall not be made the object of attack if such attack may cause the release of dangerous forces from the works or installations and consequent severe losses among the civilian population. 2. The special protection against attack provided by paragraph 1 shall cease: (a) for a dam or a dyke only if it is used for other than its normal function and in regular, significant and direct support of military operations and if such attack is the only feasible way to terminate such support; [...] 3. In all cases, the civilian population and individual civilians shall remain entitled to all the protection accorded them by international law, including the protection of the precautionary measures provided for in Article 57. If the protection ceases and any of the works, installations or military objectives mentioned in paragraph 1 is attacked, all practical precautions shall be taken to avoid the release of the dangerous forces. 4. It is prohibited to make any of the works, installations or military objectives mentioned in paragraph 1 the object of reprisals. [...] 7. In order to facilitate the identification of the objects protected by this Article, the Parties to the conflict may mark them with a special sign consisting of a group of three bright orange circles placed on the same axis, as specified in Article 16 of Annex I to this Protocol [Article 17 of Amended Annex]. The absence of such marking in no way relieves any Party to the conflict of its obligations under this Article."

31 Article 15 does not include any exception like Article 56. It reads as follows: "Works or installations containing dangerous forces, namely dams, dykes and nuclear electrical generating stations, shall not be made the object of attack, even where these objects are military objectives, if such attack may cause the release of dangerous forces and consequent severe losses among the civilian population."

installations are exempt from attacks "if such attacks may cause the release of dangerous forces and consequent severe losses among the civilian population."[32] The First and Second Protocols provide for a special regime of protection and state that dams and dykes "shall not be made the object of attack, even where these objects are military objectives."[33] The inclusion of these Articles in the Protocols represents a significant development of IHL.[34] The special protection from attack lapses, however, at least in international armed conflicts, if the dam or dyke "is used for other than its normal function and in regular, significant and direct support of military operations and if such attack is the only feasible way to terminate such support."[35]

The language of Article 56 of the First Protocol indicates that the support given to military operations must be simultaneously "regular, significant and direct."[36] Reprisals on such dams or dykes are prohibited under all circumstances. In addition, those dams and dykes that have combined functions (serving partly for irrigation and partly for electricity generation) are protected not only by Article 56, but also by Article 54 (which concerns the protection of objects indispensable to the survival of the civilian population). Therefore, an attack on such works is subject to the additional conditions imposed by paragraph 3 of Article 54, i.e. it must be limited to installations that are used only for the subsistence of combatants or otherwise in direct support of military action. Finally, in light of Article 54, attacks on dykes or dams are unlawful when they may be expected to leave so little food or water for the civilian population that it will be reduced to starvation. Therefore, by combining the principles provided in Articles 54 and 56, IHL ensures strong protection for dams and dykes in wartime.

Paragraph 3 of Article 56 of the First Protocol specifies that, in the event of significant damage to a dyke or a dam, the parties to a conflict must ensure the protection of the civilian population according to the rules of IHL. This includes the general rule contained in Article 51 on the protection of the civilian population and the precautionary measures prescribed in Article 57. In particular, the parties to a conflict must always respect the principle of proportionality between the losses inflicted and the military advantage gained from the damage inflicted on a military objective. The significance of this provision

32 Article 56.1 of the First Protocol.

33 Ibid.

34 Article 56 has been described as "a careful, thoughtful and very complex effort to balance critical humanitarian considerations against military necessity." Bothe; Partsch & Solf, supra, note 22, p. 350.

35 Article 56.2 of the First Protocol.

36 Article 56.2 (a) of the First Protocol.

is underlined by the fact that Article 85 recognizes that "an attack against works or installations containing dangerous forces in the knowledge that such attack will cause excessive loss of life, injury to civilians or damage to civilian objects"[37] constitutes a grave breach of IHL.

Implementing Article 56 of the First Protocol and Article 15 of the Second Protocol raises many challenges. As elaborated in Case Study 3, the case related to the *Armed Conflict on the Territory of the Congo* between the Democratic Republic of the Congo and Uganda illustrates the difficulties in applying Article 56 of the First Protocol to the control of dams.

During the armed conflict in the Democratic Republic of the Congo ('DRC'), Uganda's control of the Inga dam in the Congo River caused heavy losses of life among the five million inhabitants of the city of Kinshasa and the surrounding area. The DRC raised a potential violation of Article 56 of the First Protocol in its application to the International Court of Justice ('ICJ') in 1999, but it declined to pursue this argument during the written and oral phases of the proceedings before the Court. The fact that Uganda had taken control of the dam was not considered sufficient for proving a violation of Article 56 of the First Protocol.[38]

Case Study 3: Control of the Inga Dam in the Congo River.

The examples related to the Tigris, Euphrates and Congo Rivers illustrate that belligerents may seize control of dams and dykes to strengthen their hold over a territory. Controlling a dam may support the economic needs of an occupying power.

Although the importance of dams to support the energy and water needs of populations in territories under occupation may be taken for granted, IHL is surprisingly silent on this topic. The control of dams and dykes is not covered under Article 56 of the First Protocol and Article 15 of the Second Protocol. Yet, the capture of these installations may threaten the life of the local population. Control of such installations may be used to inflict suffering on the population by cutting the electricity and water supply. Moreover, the control of water installations may be used to flood farmlands and cities, exposing the population to severe losses. Article 56 of the First Protocol and Article 15 of the Second Protocol to the 1949 Geneva Conventions should be broadened in their scope of application in order to prohibit the 'control' of dams and dykes by belligerent parties.

37 Article 85.3 (c) of the First Protocol.

38 ICJ, *Armed Activities on the Territory of the Congo (Democratic Republic of the Congo* v. *Uganda), Judgment, I.C.J. Reports 2005*, p. 168, at p. 181.

The control of dams could be addressed by some specific norms included in the First Protocol. The First Protocol provides different options that merit further attention. The adoption of agreements between riparian states may be a tool to reinforce the protection of dams and dykes in international rivers. Article 56 (6) of the First Protocol indicates that states may conclude treaties to reinforce protection of these installations before or during an armed conflict. This paragraph states:

> The High Contracting Parties and the Parties to the conflict are urged to conclude further agreements among themselves to provide additional protection for objects containing dangerous forces.

The ICRC Commentary also notes that these agreements may declare dams as neutral areas supervised by international organizations.[39] The agreements concluded by the parties could set out the implementation of Article 56 (6) and bolster protection of dams and dykes. Moreover, Article 56 (7) of the First Protocol points out that dams may be identified during military operations using a special sign. This special sign may consist of a group of three bright orange circles. According to paragraph 7:

> In order to facilitate the identification of the objects protected by this article, the Parties to the conflict may mark them with a special sign consisting of a group of three bright orange circles placed on the same axis, as specified in Article 16 of Annex I to this Protocol [Article 17 of Amended Annex]. The absence of such marking in no way relieves any Party to the conflict of its obligations under this Article.

Article 17 of Annex I to the First Protocol illustrates this special sign:

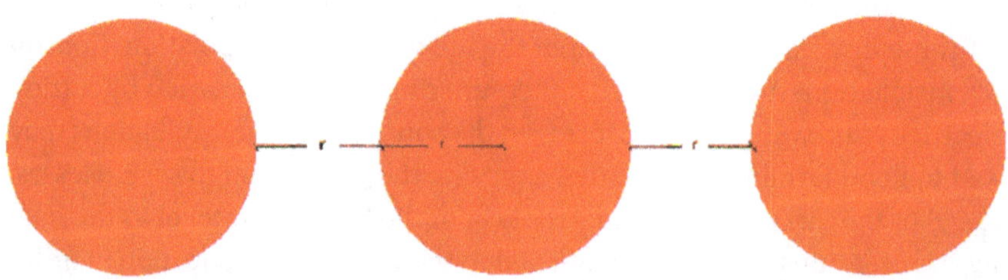

FIGURE 1 *International special sign for works and installations containing dangerous forces.*

39 Sandoz; Swinarski & Zimmerman, supra, note 7, para. 2177.

According to the Annex to the First Protocol revised in 1993:

2. The sign shall be as large as appropriate under the circumstances. When displayed over an extended surface it may be repeated as often as appropriate under the circumstances. It shall, whenever possible, be displayed on flat surfaces or on flags so as to be visible from as many directions and from as far away as possible.
3. On a flag, the distance between the outer limits of the sign and the adjacent sides of the flag shall be one radius of a circle. The flag shall be rectangular and shall have a white ground.
4. At night or when visibility is reduced, the sign may be lighted or illuminated. It may also be made of materials rendering it recognizable by technical means of detection.

Warring parties may use the three orange circles to limit the impact on dams and dykes of military operations and hinder the control of these installations during armed conflicts. Dams and dykes would be better protected if properly indicated by a distinguishable international sign.

The analysis of Articles 54 and 56 of the First Protocol shows the weaknesses of the legal protection granted to water. Water as such is not given legal protection under IHL. This area of international law protects water if this protection meets IHL's over-arching objectives of regulating the conduct of hostilities and safeguarding the civilian population. Thus, Articles 54 and 56 do not protect water specifically, but because it is a basic human need and because, depending on its use, it can become a 'weapon' against the civilian population.

Other provisions of IHL can be applied to the safeguarding of water. In particular, fresh water resources, a fundamental element of every ecosystem, must be protected by provisions applicable to the environment.

II *Water and Environmental Protection under International Humanitarian Law*

IHL has historically paid scant attention to the protection of the environment. Nevertheless, the use of a wider range of means and methods of warfare during the Vietnam War drew the attention of the international community to the need to protect it. In this context, the Stockholm Declaration of 1972 shows the rise of environmental consciousness at a global level.[40] The 1976 ENMOD

40 See Principle 26 of the Stockholm Declaration, United Nations Conference on Human Environment, UN Doc. A/CONF.48/14/REV.1 (1972).

Convention[41] and Articles 35.3 and 55 of the 1977 First Protocol mitigate the impacts of armed conflicts on the environment. These provisions contribute to preserving natural resources and form part of a body of law that protects the population and water resources.

Before analysing the specific rules protecting the environment, this monograph will analyse the general protection of the environment as a civilian object (Part 1). It will then explore the contours of the ENMOD Convention and the specific provisions of the First Protocol (Part 2).

1 The Environment as a Civilian Object

Outside of its specific rules on the protection of the environment, IHL views the environment as a civilian object.[42] The Commentary to Article 55 of the First Protocol explains that "[t]he concept of the natural environment should be understood in the widest sense to cover the biological environment in which a population is living [... It] includes forests and other vegetation [...], as well as fauna, flora and other biological or climatic elements."[43] This would then include everything that is not man-made: the atmosphere, the air, the ozone layer, the oceans and other bodies of water, soil, rocks, plants and animals. However, the very fact that the natural environment is understood in such a broad manner has created some controversy over whether it can be wholly characterized as a civilian object.

Numerous statements and declarations by states have not distinguished between parts of the environment and the environment as a whole when referring to direct attacks, destruction or incidental damage. For instance, the Final Declaration adopted by the International Conference for the Protection of War Victims of 1993 affirms "the rules of international humanitarian law applicable during armed conflicts [protect...] the natural environment, either against attacks on the environment as such or against wanton destruction causing serious environmental damage."[44] In 1992, the General Assembly stressed that

41 The ENMOD Convention is available at: https://www.icrc.org/applic/ihl/ihl.nsf/TRA/460?OpenDocument&, last accessed on 20 January 2016.

42 Karen Hulme, 'Taking Care to Protect the Environment against Damage: a Meaningless Obligation?', *International Review of the Red Cross*, Vol. 92 (879) (2010), pp. 475–691, at p. 678.

43 Sandoz; Swinarski & Zimmerman, supra, note 7, p. 661.

44 'Final Declaration for the Protection of Victims of War', *International Committee of the Red Cross* (30 August–1 September 1993), para. 10, https://www.icrc.org/eng/resources/documents/misc/57jms8.htm, last accessed on 15 October 2016.

"the destruction of the environment, not justified by military necessity and carried out wantonly, is clearly contrary to existing international law."[45]

With respect to the bombing campaign in the 1999 Kosovo war, NATO stated that, when making targeting decisions, it took into account "all possible collateral damage, be it environmental, human or to the civilian infrastructure."[46] There is therefore nothing in the practice of states that would indicate that they do not consider all of the natural environment to be protected as a civilian object. Moreover, IHL requires that everything that can be subject to an attack or destruction be classified either as a civilian object or a military objective. IHL clearly defines civilian objects as all objects which are not military objectives.[47]

Furthermore, the interplay of the proportionality principle and the specific protections contained in the First Protocol accords wide-reaching protection to the environment. Under general rules on the conduct of hostilities, the natural environment is protected against direct attack and against excessive damage. Articles 35.3 and 55 of the First Protocol have a different scope of application, setting an absolute limit to the damage that is tolerated for the environment.

2 The Prohibition on Causing Widespread, Long-Term and Severe Impacts on the Environment in Times of Armed Conflict

On 10 December 1976, the United Nations General Assembly adopted the text of the ENMOD Convention. According to this Convention, "[e]ach State Party to this Convention undertakes not to engage in military or any other hostile use of environmental modification techniques having widespread, long-lasting or severe effects as the means of destruction, damage or injury to any other State Party."[48] Its purpose is to prohibit techniques that change "the dynamics, composition or structure of the Earth."[49] A certain number of conditions must be

45 General Assembly Resolution 47/37 (25 November 1992), para. 55.

46 'Customary International Humanitarian Law Database', *International Committee of the Red Cross*, Rule 43, https://www.icrc.org/customary-ihl/eng/docs/v1_rul_rule43, last accessed on 20 January 2016.

47 Article 52.2 of the First Protocol provides the criteria to define a military objective. According to these criteria, "military objectives are limited to those objects which by their nature, location, purpose or use make an effective contribution to military action; and whose total or partial destruction, capture or neutralization, in the circumstances ruling at the time, offers a definite military advantage". See infra.

48 Article 1 of the ENMOD Convention.

49 Article 2 of the ENMOD Convention reads as follows: "As used in Article I, the term 'environmental modification techniques' refers to any technique for changing—through the deliberate manipulation of natural processes—the dynamics, composition or

met for the Convention to apply. For a technique to be prohibited, it must be employed for a "military or any other hostile use", it must have "widespread, long-lasting or severe effects", and its purpose must be "destruction, damage or injury to any other State Party."[50] A series of Understandings adopted by the parties to the Convention sets out a list of prohibited techniques, which includes tsunamis, upsets in the ecological balance of a region, and changes in weather and climate patterns. This list is not exhaustive and other phenomena could be included.[51]

The application of the ENMOD Convention depends upon bringing together several conditions that are difficult to meet simultaneously. According to the interpretation favoured by most states parties, the Convention only covers new environmental modification techniques developed after the 1970s. The United Kingdom, in particular, adopted this position in its written submissions before the ICJ in the case on the *Legality of the Threat or Use of Nuclear Weapons* in 1996.[52] However, parties to the Convention may also adopt declarations to include other specific environmental modification techniques. For example, in 1992, the Review Conference adopted a declaration adding herbicides to the list of techniques prohibited by the Convention.[53] The Review Conference may hereafter adopt further declarations to encompass other techniques that have widespread, long-lasting or serious environmental impacts.

Military strategies like river diversions are covered under the ENMOD Convention. In this regard, it is useful to note the Republic of Korea's declaration in 1986 that:

> It is the understanding of the Government of the Republic of Korea that any technique for deliberately changing the natural state of rivers falls

structure of the Earth, including its biota, lithosphere, hydrosphere and atmosphere, or of outer space."

50 Article 1 of the ENMOD Convention.

51 Understanding relating to Article II of the ENMOD Convention (10 December 1976), https://ihl-databases.icrc.org/applic/ihl/ihl.nsf/Treaty.xsp?documentId=2AC88FF62DB2CDD6C12563CD002D6EC1&action=openDocument, last accessed on 15 October 2016.

52 Letter from the Legal Advisor to the Foreign and Commonwealth Office of the United Kingdom of Great Britain and Northern Ireland, together with written comments of the United Kingdom (16 June 1995), p. 56, para. 3.76, http://www.icj-cij.org/docket/files/95/8802.pdf, last accessed on 15 October 2016.

53 *Second Review Conference of the Parties to the Convention on the Prohibition of Military or Any Other Hostile Use of Environmental Modification Techniques*, 14–22 September 1992, ENMOD/CONF.II/SR.6, pp. 11–12.

> within the meaning of the term 'environmental modification techniques' as defined in article II of the [ENMOD] Convention. It is further understood that military or any other hostile use of such techniques, which could cause flooding, inundation, reduction in the water-level, drying up, destruction of hydrotechnical installations or other harmful consequences, comes within the scope of the Convention, provided it meets the criteria set out in article I therefore.[54]

However, the inclusion of such military strategies under the ambit of the ENMOD Convention raises several problems. This instrument covers only 'high technology' strategies and its application conditions are very narrow. Moreover, the First Protocol only prohibits environmental damage that is 'widespread, long-term and severe'.

The First Protocol of 1977, adopted one year after the ENMOD Convention, aims expressly at protecting the natural environment in Articles 35.3 and 55. The ENMOD Convention and the First Protocol are complementary in times of armed conflict, prohibiting both environmental modification techniques and any methods or means of warfare that may be expected to cause widespread, long-lasting and serious damage to the environment.[55] Because these two instruments are complementary in nature, their negotiators endeavoured to use similar terms to describe the criteria that define environmental damage.

Notwithstanding the efforts of the negotiators, the ENMOD Convention and Articles 35.3 and 55 of the First Protocol[56] must be distinguished. The three adjectives used in the First Protocol to characterize environmental damage

54 *Multilateral Treaties deposited with the Secretary-General, United Nations*, 31 December 1994, p. 908, https://www.icrc.org/applic/ihl/ihl.nsf/NOTIF/460-KR?OpenDocument&, last accessed on 20 January 2016.

55 Michael Bothe, 'The Protection of the Environment in Times of Armed Conflict: Legal Rules, Uncertainty, Deficiencies and Possible Developments', *German Yearbook of International Law*, Vol. 34 (1992), pp. 54–62, at p. 57.

56 It should be noted that in its Advisory Opinion of 8 July 1996, *Legality of the Threat or Use of Nuclear Weapons*, the ICJ concluded "taken together, these provisions [Articles 35.3 and 55] embody a general obligation to protect the natural environment against widespread, long-term and severe environmental damage; the prohibition of methods and means of warfare which are intended, or may be expected, to cause such damage; and the prohibition of attacks against the natural environment by way of reprisals." The Court does not mention the environment in the operative section of its advisory opinion but draws the general conclusion that "it follows from the above-mentioned requirements that the threat or use of nuclear weapons would generally be contrary to the rules of international law applicable in armed conflict, and in particular the principles and rules of

('widespread', 'long-lasting' and 'serious') have unclear definitions.[57] Although the Understandings provide definitions for the words 'widespread', 'long-lasting' and 'severe' in the first article of the ENMOD Convention, the *travaux préparatoires* of the First Protocol indicate that the negotiators intended to attribute a different meaning to each of these three criteria.[58] According to the *travaux préparatoires*, in the First Protocol 'long-lasting' designates an effect that lasts for several decades, whereas in the ENMOD Convention 'long-lasting' means "lasting for a period of months, or approximately a season."[59] Thus, although the negotiators of the ENMOD Convention and the First Protocol chose identical terms, they attributed distinct meanings to these criteria.

Another issue arising from the criteria set out in the First Protocol is that they must be met cumulatively in order for environmental protection norms to apply. Article 35 establishes the prohibition "to employ methods or means of warfare" which can cause "widespread, long-term and severe damage to the natural environment".[60] The reference to "prejudice to the health or survival of the population" from Article 55 of the First Protocol also indicates a standard of very serious harm. The threshold of these rules is frequently criticized as it appears to be so high that in practice the rules' ability to protect the environment has been almost meaningless.[61] In other words, these cumulative

humanitarian law." ICJ, *Legality of the Threat or Use of Nuclear Weapons, Advisory Opinion, I.C.J. Reports 1996*, p. 226, at paras. 31 and 105(2)(E).

57 See Djamchid Momtaz, 'Le recours à l'arme nucléaire et la protection de l'environnement: l'apport de la Cour internationale de Justice', *in*, Laurence Boisson de Chazournes & Philippe Sands (eds.), *International Law, the International Court of Justice and Nuclear Weapons* (Cambridge University Press, 1999), pp. 354–374.

58 Alexander Kiss, 'Les Protocoles additionnels aux Conventions de Genève de 1949 et la protection des biens de l'environnement', *in*, *Études et essais sur le droit international humanitaire et sur les principes de la Croix-Rouge en l'honneur de Jean Pictet* (International Committee of the Red Cross, 1984), pp. 181–192.

59 Understandings regarding the Convention related to Article I of the ENMOD Convention, https://www.icrc.org/applic/ihl/ihl.nsf/xsp/.ibmmodres/domino/OpenAttachment/applic/ihl/ihl.nsf/2AC88FF62DB2CDD6C12563CD002D6EC1/FULLTEXT/IHL-70-EN.pdf, last accessed on 20 January 2016.

60 'Long-term' is understood to refer to decades, 'widespread' is understood to refer to several hundred square kilometres and 'severe' means a serious disruption of the ecosystem or in relation to Article 55 refers to the prejudice to the health or survival of the population. Sandoz; Swinarski & Zimmerman, supra, note 7, p. 414.

61 Michal Bothe; Carl Bruch; Jordan Diamond & David Jensen, 'International Law Protecting the Environment during Armed Conflict: Gaps and Opportunities', *International Review of the Red Cross*, Vol. 92 (879) (2010), pp. 569–602, at p. 576.

impacts imply that these norms only protect the environment against catastrophic events or 'ecocides'.

The International Committee of the Red Cross emphasized that "the question as to what constitutes (prohibited) 'widespread, severe or long-term' damage and what is acceptable damage to the environment is open to interpretation."[62] As one author has remarked, however, "[w]hat would be considered as excessive environmental damage is not clear, and it is not static over time. What was considered as acceptable collateral damage decades, or even years ago, that is proportionate to the military advantage pursued, might not be regarded as acceptable today."[63] In the context of water resources, this statement is particularly true. Nowadays the vital importance and vulnerability of water resources, especially in times of armed conflict, is accentuated by water scarcity and the risks of drought in many regions of the world. While water, together with the rest of the environment, may suffer from pollution and degradation when relations between states are peaceful, the problem is far worse in time of war, when contamination may be deliberate rather than accidental.

Furthermore, a unique feature of environmental damage to water resources is that its impact frequently extends over large areas for years or even decades after the end of a war. This has severe consequences for the civilian population and can even lead to the displacement of entire communities, which in itself can cause stress on water resources.[64] The nature, scope and implications of the negative environmental consequences of war have been well documented in the series of Post-Conflict Environmental Assessments published by UNEP which have significantly contributed to raising awareness of the problem.[65]

---

62 Protection of the Natural Environment in Time of Armed Conflict, Contribution of the International Committee of the Red Cross to the Rio Conference (June 1992), https://www.icrc.org/eng/resources/documents/report/5deesv.htm, last accessed on 15 October 2016.

63 Richard Desgagne, 'The Prevention of Environmental Damage in Time of Armed Conflict: Proportionality and Precautionary Measures', *Yearbook of International Humanitarian Law*, Vol. 3 (2000), pp. 109–129, at p. 119.

64 'The Democratic Republic of Congo, Post-Conflict Environmental Assessment, Synthesis for Policy Makers', *United Nations Environment Programme* (*UNEP*) (2011), p. 26, http://postconflict.unep.ch/publications/UNEP_DRC_PCEA_EN.pdf, last accessed on 15 October 2016.

65 See 'The Post-Conflict Environmental Assessments on the Democratic Republic of Congo', *UNEP* (2011); 'Sudan', *UNEP* (2007, 2008); 'Lebanon', *UNEP* (2007); 'Iraq', *UNEP* (2007); 'Afghanistan', *UNEP* (2003, 2011); 'Occupied Palestinian Territories', *UNEP* (2003, 2006,

As illustrated by Case Study 4, the threshold of Articles 35 and 55 of the First Protocol is so high that in practice the rules' ability to protect the environment has been almost meaningless.

> The practical difficulties involved in applying the high and imprecise threshold of Articles 35.3 and 55 of the First Protocol are illustrated by the 2000 decision of the Committee of the International Criminal Tribunal for the former Yugoslavia ('ICTY'). The Committee was tasked with examining whether any evidence justified opening an investigation into NATO's air campaign against the Federal Republic of Yugoslavia ('FRY'); in completing this task, the Committee analysed the content of Articles 35.3 and 55 of the First Protocol. Unfortunately, the Committee recommended that the Office of the Prosecutor not open an investigation into environmental damages and noted that the three conditions required by the First Protocol could only be met simultaneously under extreme circumstances. The Committee reasoned that NATO did not have enough information on the bombed sites for the Office of the Prosecutor to open an investigation. The Committee's reasoning on this point, however, is inconsistent. Indeed, after stating that "the targeting [...] of Serbian petro-chemical industries may well have served a clear and important military purpose," it asserted that it was doubtful that NATO "could [...] have reasonably expected that toxic chemicals of the sort allegedly released into the environment by the bombing campaign would be stored alongside that military target."[66] According to the Committee, NATO was able to determine the strategic value of the targeted factories on the banks of the Danube but did not have enough information to assess the risks these attacks would pose to water resources.

Case Study 4: Final Report to the Prosecutor by the Committee Established to Review the NATO Bombing Campaign against the Federal Republic of Yugoslavia.

There are other cases that have raised the issue of the relationship between environmental protection and humanitarian law. The Eritrea-Ethiopia Claims Commission touched upon this issue, as discussed further in Case Study 5.

2009); 'Kosovo', *UNEP & United Nations Centre for Human Settlements (UNCHS)* (1999), http://www.unep.org/disastersandconflicts/Publications/tabid/54718/Default.aspx, last accessed on 20 January 2016.

66 *Final Report to the Prosecutor by the Committee established to Review the NATO Bombing Campaign against the Federal Republic of Yugoslavia*, June 2000, paras. 15, 17 and 22–25, http://www.icty.org/sid/10052, last accessed on 20 January 2016.

The two-year war between Eritrea and Ethiopia resulted in extensive environmental damage. Ethiopia argued that Eritrean forces had destroyed gum arabic and resin plants and caused the loss of trees and seedlings. The Commission, however, rejected the Ethiopian allegations and stated that the evidence of destruction of environmental resources fell well below the standard of widespread and long-lasting environmental damage required under IHL.[67]

Case Study 5: Eritrea-Ethiopia Claims Commission.

Notwithstanding the Eritrea-Ethiopian example, the illegal exploitation of natural resources may rise to a violation of IHL. Rules regarding enemy property may be interpreted as protecting natural resources in occupied territory to the extent that these resources constitute the "property of the enemy" under the Convention (IV) respecting the Laws and Customs of War on Land and its Annex: Regulations concerning the Laws and Customs of War on Land of 1907 (The Hague Regulations of 1907) and the 1949 Convention (IV) on the Protection of Civilian Persons in Time of War (the Fourth Geneva Convention). These two instruments prohibit the looting of both private and public property in occupied territories.[68] Case Study 6 shows how these principles were applied in a dispute between Uganda and the Democratic Republic of the Congo.

Thus, judicial bodies have taken into account the explicit or implicit connections between armed conflict and environmental protection, as shown in the case between Eritrea and Ethiopia brought to a Commission established under the auspices of the PCA and the judgment concerning the DRC of the International Court of Justice. In the *Eritrea/Ethiopia* case, the destruction of gum arabic and resin plants and the military operations of Eritrea had an impact on the trees and seedlings in Ethiopia. These attacks affected the living conditions of the population and their access to food. Moreover, in the DRC, the looting and systematic exploitation of natural resources had an impact on human rights putting in danger the life of the population in the DRC. The connections between the environment and conflicts should be considered in light of the protection of the civilian population. For example, the illegal exploitation and depletion of groundwater resources may be sanctioned in parallel by the prohibition to attack objects indispensable to the survival of the civilian

67 PCA, *Eritrea-Ethiopia Claims Commission—Partial Award: Central Front—Ethiopia's Claim 2*, Decision of 28 April 2004, *Reports of International Arbitral Awards*, Vol. XXVI, para. 100.

68 Specifically, Article 47 of The Hague Regulations of 1907 and Article 33 of the Fourth Geneva Convention.

population and Articles 35.3 and 55 of the First Protocol on the protection of the environment and the prohibition of looting natural resources.

A violation of the 1907 Hague Regulations and the 1949 Fourth Geneva Convention was invoked by the DRC in its case against Uganda before the ICJ. In this case, the DRC argued that Ugandan troops had engaged in looting and the systematic exploitation of its natural resources. The Court relied, on the one hand, on the report of the Judicial Commission of Inquiry Into Allegations of Illegal Exploitation of Natural Resources and Other Forms of Wealth in DRC, chaired by Justice David Porter, and, on the other hand, on the reports of the United Nations Panels of Experts on Illegal Resource Exploitation in the DRC to conclude that where the Ugandan troops were involved in the "looting, plundering and exploitation of natural resources in the territory of the DRC", the rules of IHL were breached, including Article 47 of the Hague Regulations of 1907 and Article 33 of the Fourth Geneva Convention. Uganda was required to monitor the use of natural resources by its armed forces in order to prevent and punish such exploitation.[69]

Case Study 6: Democratic Republic of the Congo v. Uganda at the ICJ.

The prohibition on causing widespread, long-lasting and serious damage enshrined in Articles 35.3 and 55 of the First Protocol of 1977 is part of a body of rules applicable only to international armed conflicts. Non-international armed conflicts and territories under military occupation are not, however, free from any legal constraints with regard to natural resources.[70] The ICJ recalled that "[S]tates must take environmental considerations into account when assessing what is necessary and proportionate in the pursuit of

69 ICJ, *Armed Activities on the Territory of the Congo (Democratic Republic of the Congo* v. *Uganda), Judgment, I.C.J. Reports 2005*, p. 168, paras. 242–245.

70 In this regard, it should be recalled that the 'Guidelines for Military Manuals and Instructions on the Protection of the Environment in Times of Armed Conflict' of 1996 encourage parties to non-international armed conflict "to apply the same rules that provide protection of the environment in international armed conflict". The Guidelines have been annexed to a resolution adopted by the UN General Assembly that invites all States to "give due consideration to the possibility of incorporating [the Guidelines] into their military manuals and other instructions addressed to their military personnel." (GA/RES/49/50, 9 December 1994). *International Review of the Red Cross*, No. 311 (1996), https://www.icrc.org/eng/resources/documents/article/other/57jn38.htm, last accessed on 15 October 2016.

legitimate military objectives."[71] The principles of necessity and proportionality must incorporate environmental considerations. This being said, the lack of specific provisions on the environment in the Second Protocol is a major weakness of the legal regime applicable to non-international armed conflicts. The law governing non-international armed conflicts does not establish a clear threshold for prohibited environmental damage. This uncertainty may make it difficult in practice to ensure effective protection. Likewise, it is unclear to what extent parties to such conflicts are required to adopt precautions in the conduct of military operations in order to avoid or minimize incidental damage to the environment. Given that the majority of armed conflicts today are non-international, these legal uncertainties warrant urgent attention. General principles of IHL may partially counter the lack of protection of the environment during non-international armed conflicts.

III *General Principles of International Humanitarian Law and the Protection of Water Resources*

In addition to the environmental protection norms contained in the First Protocol and the special protection of water infrastructure under the First and Second Protocols, the monograph considers the obligations that flow indirectly from the general principles of IHL, which govern the law applicable both to international and non-international armed conflicts. These principles must be taken into account when interpreting the rules that apply specifically to water, such as the prohibition on attacking dams, dykes, and objects indispensable to the survival of the civilian population. Jean Pictet, one of the main architects of IHL, underlined the importance of the general principles of IHL. He argued that "international conventions are made up of a multitude of rules that set out the specific obligations of States", but that some principles inspire all regulation of armed conflicts. Sometimes these principles are "explicitly stated", but at other times "they are implicit and express the substance" of the regulation. In some cases, "they also result from custom".[72] Some of the most fundamental principles of the law of armed conflict are the principles of humanity, distinction, proportionality and precaution in attack.[73]

71 ICJ, *Legality of the Threat or Use of Nuclear Weapons, Advisory Opinion, I.C.J. Reports 1996*, p. 226, at para. 30.

72 Jean Pictet, *Development and Principles of International Humanitarian Law. Course given in July 1982 at the University of Strasbourg as part of the courses organized by the International Institute of Human Rights* (Martinus Nijhoff Publishers, 1982), p. 73.

73 The principle of military necessity is not addressed in the present contribution. On this topic see: Tignino (2011), supra, note 4, pp. 25–29.

1 The Martens Clause

The Martens clause may support interpretations of IHL norms that strengthen the protection of water resources. The clause underscores the importance of an evolutionary reading of the rules of IHL in light of the principle of humanity and the dictates of public conscience. These are increasingly understood to include environmental concerns.[74] Indeed, as already noted, as international concern for environmental protection has grown over the past twenty years, the need to ensure such protection during armed conflicts has gained more support.

The Martens clause affirms that in those situations not covered by conventional law, "civilians and combatants remain under the protection and authority of the principles of international law derived from established custom, from the principles of humanity and from the dictates of public conscience."[75] Principles of humanity may play a significant role in the protection of the environment. In this regard, the 1996 'Guidelines for Military Manuals and Instructions on the Protection of the Environment in Times of Armed Conflict' explicitly state that "[i]n cases not covered by international agreements, the environment remains under the protection and authority of the principles of international law derived from established custom, the principles of humanity and the dictates of public conscience."[76]

Experts have divided views on the proper interpretation of the Martens clause and its normative function *per se*.[77] In light of the doctrinal sources, one

74 Cordula Droege & Marie-Louise Tougas, 'The Protection of the Natural Environment in Armed Conflict—Existing Rules and Need for Further Legal Protection', *Nordic Journal of International Law*, Vol. 82 (2013), pp. 21–52, p. 40.

75 Article 1.2 of the First Protocol. See also Article 63 of the Geneva Convention for the Amelioration of the Condition of the Wounded and Sick in Armed Forces in the Field (Geneva Convention I), 12 August 1949; Article 62 of the Geneva Convention for the Amelioration of the Condition of the Wounded, Sick and Shipwrecked Members of Armed Forces at Sea (Geneva Convention II), 12 August 1949; Article 142 of the Geneva Convention on Prisoners of War (Geneva Convention III), 12 August 1949; Article 158 of the Geneva Convention relative to the Protection of Civilian Persons in Time of War (Geneva Convention IV), 12 August 1949.

76 'Guidelines for Military Manuals and Instructions on the Protection of the Environment in Times of Armed Conflict', *International Review of the Red Cross*, No. 311 (1996), para. 7, https://www.icrc.org/eng/resources/documents/article/other/57jn38.htm, last accessed on 15 October 2016.

77 Singh and McWhinney affirm that "the supreme intention of the Martens clause is to negate any possibility of the omitted questions, not covered by written rules, being left to the arbitrary opinion of military commanders." Nagendra Singh & Edward McWhinney, *Nuclear Weapons and Contemporary International Law* (2nd ed., Martinus

can say that there is no unified interpretation of the Martens clause and that international lawyers have different understandings of its scope.[78] According to the strictest interpretation, the Martens clause serves "as a reminder that customary international humanitarian law continues to apply after the adoption of a treaty."[79] According to the ICRC Commentary, however, the Martens clause has a broader scope of application since it prevents everything that is not expressly prohibited by treaties from being allowed during armed conflicts.[80]

The Martens clause must be analysed in conjunction with the principle of humanity. The norms of IHL law are inspired, on the one hand, by this principle, and on the other, by military needs. IHL tries to achieve a balance between these two requirements. In the case regarding the *Corfu Channel*, the ICJ stated that Albania's obligations were based "on certain general and well-recognized principles, namely: elementary considerations of humanity."[81] Moreover, in its judgment concerning *Military and Paramilitary Activities in and Against Nicaragua*, the ICJ expressed the view that certain rules which stated in common Article 3 of the 1949 Geneva Conventions are "rules which, in the Court's opinion, reflect what the Court in 1949 called 'elementary considerations of

Nijhoff Publishers, 1989), pp. 46–47. According to Schwarzemberg, the goal of the clause is "[to] forestall an unintended and cynical argument *a contrario*. Because the [Hague] Regulations on Law Warfare were not exhaustive, the Parties wished to avoid the interpretation that anything that was not expressly prohibited by these Regulations was allowed." Georg Schwarzemberg, *The Legality of Nuclear Weapons* (Stevens and Sons, 1958), pp. 10–11. Meron considers that "prohibitions could arise by and be generally binding by virtue of general principles of international law and of humanity [...]. The clause was seen as providing that actions that are not explicitly prohibited by treaty or customary rule are not *ipso facto* permitted and that the conduct of the parties to a conflict is judged not only in accordance with treaties and custom, but also in light of the principles of international law referred to in the clause." Theodor Meron, 'The Martens Clause, Principles of Humanity and Dictates of Public Conscience', *American Journal of International Law*, Vol. 94 (2000), p. 86.

78 Rupert Ticehurst, 'La clause de Martens et le droit des conflits armés', *International Review of the Red Cross*, No. 824 (1997), pp. 133–142. See also Antonio Cassese, 'The Martens Clause: Half a Loaf or Simply Pie in the Sky?', *European Journal of International Law*, Vol. 11(1) (2000), pp. 189–192.

79 Christopher Greenwood, 'Historical Development and Legal Basis', *in*, Dieter Fleck (ed.), *The Handbook of International Humanitarian Law* (Oxford University Press, 2008), p. 35, para. 130.

80 Sandoz; Swinarski & Zimmerman, supra, note 7, p. 39. See also Singh & McWhinney, supra, note 77, pp. 46–47; Meron, supra, note 77, p. 86.

81 ICJ, *Corfu Channel case, Judgment of April 9th, 1949: I.C.J. Reports 1949*, p. 4, at p. 22.

humanity.'"[82] In light of the jurisprudence of the International Court of Justice, Judge Mohammed Shahabuddeen affirmed that the Martens clause

> provided its own self-sufficient and conclusive authority for the proposition that there were already in existence principles of international law under which considerations of humanity could themselves exert legal force to govern military conduct in cases in which no relevant rule was provided by conventional law.[83]

Taking into account both the elementary considerations of humanity and the dictates of public conscience affirmed in the Martens clause, the norms of IHL could be interpreted in a manner that strengthens the protection of water resources. The principles and norms of IHL must be read in the context of general international law and in conjunction with the evolution of other areas of international law. The Martens clause may be a tool for reading the rules of IHL in a dynamic way,[84] by taking into account principles of general international law like the right to life. The principle of humanity is based on the dignity of human beings. The protection of the human right to life, which includes the right to a dignified existence and the protection of basic human needs, are part of that principle. Cutting water supplies or poisoning drinking water sources constitute a breach of the right to life and indiscriminately impact combatants and the civilian population.

2 The Principle of Proportionality and the Obligation to Take Precautionary Measures

The application of general principles of IHL can play a role with regard to the minimization of environmental harm.[85] These principles may lower the threshold required by Articles 35.3 and 55 of the First Protocol and fill the gaps of environmental protection provisions during non-international armed conflicts. The ICRC Study on Customary International Humanitarian Law

---

82 ICJ, *Military and Paramilitary Activities in and against Nicaragua (Nicaragua* v. *United States of America), Merits, Judgment, I.C.J. Reports 1986*, p. 14, at para. 218.

83 *Dissenting opinion of Mohammed Shahabuddeen, I.C.J. Reports 1996*, p. 408.

84 In this regard, it has been argued that "the Martens Clause allows for a flexible interpretation of humanitarian rules, notably by authorizing the interpreter to have recourse to interpretative tools" such as human rights law. Giovanni Di Stefano & Etienne Henry, 'Final Provisions, including the Martens Clause', *in*, Andrew Clapham; Paola Gaeta & Marco Sassòli (eds.), *The 1949 Geneva Conventions. A Commentary* (Oxford University Press, 2015), pp. 155–190, at pp. 185–186.

85 Desgagne, supra, note 63, pp. 109–129, at p. 113.

affirms that "[t]he general principles on the conduct of hostilities apply to the natural environment."[86] This rule of environmental protection applies in both international and non-international armed conflicts.[87] Moreover, in the conduct of military operations, "all feasible precautions must be taken to avoid, and in any event to minimize, incidental damage to the environment. Lack of scientific certainty as to the effects on the environment of certain military operations does not absolve a party to the conflict from taking such precautions."[88]

a *Dual-use Targets*

Hostilities are increasingly taking place in urban environments, and the development of weaponry over the last several decades has heightened the risk of extensive and indiscriminate attacks on civilian objects. The use of weapons such as missiles, rockets, and mortars causes severe damage to water supplies and electricity grids. The use of heavy explosive weapons in cities often violates the rules of war and exposes civilians to unnecessary risk. For example, past experience has shown that, if an electricity network is targeted by an adversary as a military objective, damage to electricity networks can lead to serious disruption of sewage and waste water treatment systems and in turn seriously harm water and soil quality. This damage may be foreseeable and should be taken into account in a proportionality assessment.

In the last decades, the interconnections between electricity, water supplies and public health have been increasingly recognized in protracted conflicts in urban settings.[89] Electricity plays an essential role in providing access to water supplies to the population. Although electrical facilities are protected under the rules dealing with civilian objects during international and non-international armed conflicts, these norms are uncertain and in need of clarification. In particular, electrical facilities have often been considered as 'dual-use' objects. As illustrated by Case Study 7, this means that electrical facilities may have a dual function and may be used for the civilian population, but also for military purposes.

During armed conflicts power plants have been the object of military attacks, as illustrated in Case Study 8 on the conflict between Ethiopia and Eritrea.

86 International Committee of the Red Cross, Customary International Humanitarian Law Database, Rule 43, https://www.icrc.org/customary-ihl/eng/docs/v1_rul_rule43, last accessed on 20 January 2016.

87 Ibid.

88 Ibid., Rule 44.

89 Dross et al., supra, note 6.

The Committee established by the Prosecutor of the International Criminal Tribunal for the former Yugoslavia (ICTY), in charge of verifying whether there was a sufficient basis to proceed with an investigation regarding the air campaign by NATO against the Former Republic of Yugoslavia, examined the issue of the protection of objects with a 'dual-use'. In this regard, the report of the Committee points out that "opinions may differ" in relation to "dual-use objects that have some civilian uses and some actual or potential military use."[90]

Case Study 7: Final Report to the Prosecutor by the Committee Established to Review the NATO Bombing Campaign against the Federal Republic of Yugoslavia.

The Eritrea-Ethiopia Claims Commission has examined attacks against a power station in Eritrea. Ethiopian forces dropped several bombs that hit and seriously damaged the plant of Hirgigo. Eritrea asserted that the bombing of the plant was unlawful because the plant was not a legitimate military objective. Ethiopia rejected this claim and affirmed that, at the time of the attack, the Hirgigo plant was not an electrical facility, but rather a base for anti-aircraft missile launchers. The Commission, by a majority, found that, according to the circumstances prevailing at the time of the attack, "the Hirgigo power station was a military objective, as defined in Article 52, paragraph 2, of Geneva Protocol I and that Ethiopia's aerial bombardment of it was not unlawful."

However, this finding of the Commission has been criticized by the President of the Commission, Hans Van Houtte, who observed that the reasons evoked by Ethiopia do not meet the criteria established under the First Protocol. According to Van Houtte, a civilian object used for the military becomes a military objective only if it makes "an effective contribution to military action" and gives "a substantial, specific and immediate military advantage." The contribution to military action should be assessed in an objective and concrete way and not *in abstracto*. The President of the Commission affirmed that: "The Hirgigo power station, which was intended to become a principal supplier of electricity in Eritrea, unquestionably had a civilian purpose. It could have been a military objective if it was established

90 Final Report to the Prosecutor by the Committee Established to Review the NATO Bombing Campaign against the Federal Republic of Yugoslavia, 2000, para. 37, http://www.icty.org/en/press/final-report-prosecutor-committee-established-review-nato-bombing-campaign-against-federal, last accessed on 15 October 2016.

that it made or could make an effective contribution to military action, or was or could be of fundamental importance for the conduct of war. A determination that the Hirgigo power station was a military objective must sufficiently specify the basis for this assumption."[91]

The opinion of the President of the Eritrea-Ethiopia Claims Commission supports the principle that military objectives are limited to those objects which make an effective contribution to military action.

Case Study 8: Eritrea-Ethiopia Claims Commission.

Another example of targeting dual-use objects is related to the attacks against the Jiyeh power plant in Beirut during the 2006 Lebanon war, discussed below in Case Study 9.[92]

91 PCA, *Eritrea-Ethiopia Claims Commission—Partial Award: Western Front, Aerial Bombardment and Related Claims—Eritrea's Claims 1, 3, 5, 9–13, 14, 21, 25 & 26*, Decision of 19 December 2005, *Reports of International Arbitral Awards*, Vol. XXVI, pp. 329–330, paras. 106–121 and dissenting opinion, http://legal.un.org/riaa/cases/vol_XXVI/291-349.pdf, last accessed on 15 October 2016.

92 Industrial facilities are another illustration of 'dual-use' objects. During the war in Yugoslavia, the attacks against industrial facilities near the Danube River caused significant damage to water resources. The bombing of the Pancevo industrial complex and a petroleum refinery in Novi Sad by NATO forces during the war in Kosovo contributed to the release of some 80,000 tons of crude oil into the soil and of many tons of other toxic substances. Groundwater resources near the town were polluted. The UNEP/UNCHS Balkan Task Force reported that after the bombing of the industrial site, two water wells providing water to Novi Sad were closed and around 50,000 people were deprived of safe water. The Task Force recommended taking urgent measures to ensure safe drinking water. The conflict's impact on the environment was clearly "excessive in relation to the concrete and direct military advantage anticipated" and constitutes a violation of Article 57.2 (a) (iii) of the First Protocol on precautionary measures. Final Report to the Prosecutor by the Committee Established to Review the NATO Bombing Campaign against the Federal Republic of Yugoslavia, 2000, para. 37, http://www.icty.org/en/press/final-report-prosecutor-committee-established-review-nato-bombing-campaign-against-federal, last accessed on 15 October 2016.

The attacks on 13 and 15 July 2006 against the power plant in Beirut led to the release of an estimated 12,000 to 15,000 tons of fuel into the Mediterranean Sea and the contamination of groundwater resources and soils. The oil spill affected approximately 150 kilometres of Lebanon's coast. On 5 August 2006, Lebanon formally requested UNEP to conduct a post-conflict environmental assessment on the conflict. The scope of UNEP's assessment work was limited to Lebanon. Coastal communities have been severely affected by the oil pollution caused by the bombing of the power plant. During and in the immediate aftermath of the conflict, the government worked jointly with international organizations in an effort to contain the oil spill and implement clean-up measures along the Lebanese coast. (UNEP, Environmental Post Conflict Assessment, 2006, pp. 42–49).

The Human Rights Council decided to establish the UN Inquiry Commission on Lebanon. This Commission addressed the issue of environmental damage for the first time, pointing out:

> [...] the devastating effect the oil spill from the bombing of the Jiyyeh power plant has had and will continue to have in the years to come. The Commission is convinced that this attack was premeditated. The spill affected two thirds of Lebanon's coastline. IDF's [Israeli Defence Force] failure to take the necessary precautionary measures violated Israel's obligations to protect the natural environment and the right to health. In particular, it caused significant damage to the Byblos archaeological site, included in the UNESCO World Heritage list (A/HRC/3/2, 2006 para. 23).

In December 2006, the UN General Assembly adopted a resolution on the "Oil Slick on Lebanese Shores" which recognized that the attacks by IDF's forces caused an "environmental disaster" and the oil slick covered "the entirety of the Lebanese coastline and extended beyond."[93] Moreover, the resolution, in noting that the oil slick had heavily polluted the shores of Lebanon, indicated the "serious implications for human health, biodiversity, fisheries and tourism, all four of which in turn have serious implications for livelihoods and the economy of Lebanon". It added that Israel should "assume responsibility for prompt and adequate compensation to the Government of Lebanon for the costs of repairing the environmental damage caused by the destruction, including the restoration of the marine environment" and called on the international financial institutions and international organizations to "provide financial and technical assistance to the Government of Lebanon in support of its efforts to clean up the polluted shores and sea of Lebanon with a view to preserving its ecosystem".

93 UN General Assembly Resolution 61/194 (20 December 2006), paras. 1–4.

This resolution represents an important step forward in enhancing environmental protection in times of armed conflicts. It provides for the principle of compensation for the costs incurred in reparation of environmental damage caused by an intentional attack during an armed conflict.

Case Study 9: The War in Lebanon.

There is an increasing need to clarify the rules applicable to power plants. The provisions of international humanitarian law should be read in an integrated manner, taking into account the relationship between several rules of IHL. For instance, the protection of electrical facilities can be read together with the rules on "objects indispensable to the survival of the civilian population."[94]

In conflict-affected areas, an electrical facility could play a key role in providing water indispensable for the life of the civilian population and ensuring public health. Article 54 of the First Protocol and Article 14 of the Second Protocol provide an illustrative list of the "objects indispensable to the survival of the civilian population". It is suggested that this list could be expanded to include electrical facilities. A report of Human Rights Watch has underscored:

> Insofar as the civilian population is concerned, it makes little or no difference whether a drinking water facility is attacked and destroyed, or is made inoperable by the destruction of the electrical plant supplying its power. In either case, civilians suffer the same effects—they are denied the use of a public utility indispensable for their survival.[95]

Considering electrical facilities as "objects indispensable to the survival of the civilian population"[96] may play a significant role in strengthening their protection.

During armed conflicts, electrical facilities constitute civilian objects and as such they are protected under IHL. Article 52 of the First Protocol provides:

> Civilian objects shall not be the object of attack or reprisals. Civilian objects are all objects which are not military objectives as defined in paragraph 2.

94 Article 54 of the First Protocol and Article 14 of the Second Protocol.

95 Human Rights Watch, *Needless Deaths in the Gulf War. Civilian Casualties During the Air Campaign and Violations of the Laws of War*, 1991, Chapter IV, Section C, available at: https://www.hrw.org/reports/pdfs/u/us/us.910/us910full.pdf.

96 Article 56 of the First Protocol and Article 14 of the Second Protocol.

Paragraph 2 of this Article adds:

> Attacks shall be limited strictly to military objectives. In so far as objects are concerned, military objectives are limited to those objects which by their nature, location, purpose or use make an effective contribution to military action and whose total or partial destruction, capture or neutralization, in the circumstances ruling at the time, offer a definite military advantage.

In contrast to the First Protocol, the Second Protocol does not contain a specific provision dealing with the protection of civilian objects. However, this does not mean that these objects are not protected during non-international armed conflicts. Article 13 (1) of the Second Protocol covers civilian objects, in its affirmation that:

1. The civilian population and individual civilians shall enjoy general protection against the dangers arising from military operations. To give effect to this protection, the following rules shall be observed in all circumstances.
2. The civilian population as such, as well as individual civilians, shall not be the object of attack. Acts or threats of violence the primary purpose of which is to spread terror among the civilian population are prohibited.

This Article has been interpreted as covering the protection of civilian objects during non-international armed conflicts.[97]

b *Precautionary Measures*

Attacks on military targets may cause incidental damage, known as 'collateral damage',[98] that may harm the environment. On this issue, it may be recalled that the First Protocol prohibits attacks that cause "incidental loss of civilian life, […] damage to civilian objects, or a combination thereof, which would be excessive in relation to the concrete and direct military advantage anticipated."[99] When an attack is launched, therefore, the warring parties have a duty to

97 According to Rule 7 of customary humanitarian law: "The parties to the conflict must at all times distinguish between civilian objects and military objectives. Attacks may only be directed against military objectives. Attacks must not be directed against civilian objects." Available at: https://www.icrc.org/customary-ihl/eng/docs/v1_rul_rule7.

98 Bothe; Partsch & Solf, supra, note 22, pp. 577–578.

99 Article 57.2 (a) (iii) of the First Protocol.

assess whether this attack risks causing damages that are "excessive in relation to the concrete and direct military advantage anticipated."[100] Environmental harm can amount to 'excessive' damage. It may, however, be difficult to define the precise contours of such damages. Incorporating environmental considerations into the principle of proportionality, however, acts as a counterweight to military requirements by assessing the environmental impact of an attack. This principle is one aspect of the founding concept of IHL, which states that warring parties do not have unlimited rights to choose methods and means of warfare.

The First Protocol mandates taking precautionary measures in the conduct of hostilities and requires that "constant care [...] be taken to spare the civilian population, civilians and civilian objects."[101] Thus, the means and methods of warfare must be used with due regard to the protection and preservation of the environment.[102] A party to a conflict must take all feasible precautions in choosing means and methods of warfare with a view to avoiding and minimizing incidental impact on the environment as a civilian object.[103] Moreover, when a choice is to be made between several military objectives that would yield a similar military advantage, the objective selected must be the one on which the attack may be expected to cause the least danger to the environment.[104]

Human beings depend on the environment for their livelihood and well-being, in some cases even for their survival. However, international rules protecting the environment in armed conflicts are either absent or insufficient.[105] The adoption of precautionary measures by warring parties may contribute to the protection of water resources. The precautionary principle is recognized in international environmental law and in international water law.[106] By acting in accordance with this principle, warring parties can anticipate the risk of

---

100 Ibid.

101 Article 57.2.

102 International Committee of the Red Cross, Customary International Humanitarian Law Database, Rule 44, https://ihl-databases.icrc.org/customary-ihl/eng/docs/v1_rul_rule44, last accessed on 15 October 2016.

103 Article 57.2 (a) (ii) of the First Protocol.

104 Article 57.3 of the First Protocol.

105 31st International Conference of the Red Cross and Red Crescent (Geneva, 28 November–1 December 2011), Draft Resolution and Report, 'Strengthening Legal Protection for Victims of Armed Conflicts', pp. 14–17, https://www.icrc.org/eng/assets/files/red-cross-crescent-movement/31st-international-conference/31-int-conference-strengthening-legal-protection-11-5-1-1-en.pdf, last accessed on 15 October 2016.

106 See, for example, Principle 15 of the Rio Declaration on the Environment and Development (1992). Article 12 of the International Law Commission's Draft Articles on Transboundary

damaging water resources. Furthermore, the lack of scientific certainty cannot be used as an excuse for neglecting measures that could avoid harm to the environment. In IHL, the precautionary principle provides an objective criterion for the assessment of collateral damage to the environment in order to avoid or minimize it. As stated by Bothe: "the [ICRC] Study [on customary IHL] rightly acknowledges that [...] the general customary law development of the precautionary principle in international environmental law cannot be imagined to have left out the laws of armed conflict."[107] This principle introduces the notion of scientific uncertainty into warring parties' assessment of means and methods of warfare that risk causing widespread, long-term and severe damage to the environment. The obligation to take precautionary measures, even where scientific uncertainty subsists, protects water resources in both international and non-international armed conflicts.

3 The Principles of Discrimination and Distinction

Cutting drinking water supplies threatens civilian lives and may spread terror among the population. The principle of discrimination requires that military attacks be directed at specific military objectives. Its very nature therefore requires drawing a distinction between military objectives and civilian objects. The prohibition of indiscriminate attacks covers the use of weapons whose effects are uncontrollable and are likely to strike military objectives and civilian objects without distinction. The use in densely populated areas of weapons that cannot be directed at a military objective with sufficient precision is likely to result in indiscriminate attacks and is prohibited.[108]

The principle of discrimination is closely related to the principle of distinction.[109] Both play a significant role in limiting the impacts of armed conflicts on water. However, in modern conflicts, the distinction between military

---

Aquifers, Official Records of the General Assembly, Sixty-third session, Supplement No. 10 (A/63/10), (2008).

107 M. Bothe, 'Customary International Humanitarian Law: Some Reflections on the ICRC Study', *Yearbook of International Humanitarian Law*, Vol. 8 (2007), p. 107.

108 International Committee of the Red Cross, Customary International Humanitarian Law Database, Rules 11 and 12, https://www.icrc.org/customary-ihl/eng/docs/v1_rul_rule11 and https://www.icrc.org/customary-ihl/eng/docs/v1_rul_rule12, last accessed on 20 January 2016.

109 Article 48.1 of the First Protocol requires that: "In order to ensure respect for and protection of the civilian population and civilian objects, the Parties to the conflict shall at all times distinguish between the civilian population and combatants and between civilian objects and military objectives and accordingly shall direct their operations only against military objectives."

targets and civilian objects can be blurred. Attacks carried out against dual-use objects, such as industrial sites, electrical facilities or bridges used for civil and military purposes, are likely to have indirect impacts on water.

Attacks must be restricted to military targets. Article 52 of the First Protocol defines military objectives as "those objects which by their own nature, location, purpose or use make an effective contribution to military action and whose total or partial destruction, capture or neutralization, in the circumstances ruling at the time, offers a definite military advantage."[110] 'Nature' refers to the intrinsic character of an object. No part of the environment is a military objective by nature. However, according to these criteria, in a given military situation, parts of the environment may make an effective contribution to military action by virtue of their particular location, their purpose or their present use.[111] For example, because of its location, a hill can become a military objective if there is a military need to seize it or to prevent the enemy from seizing it. On the other hand, it is difficult to see how an international watercourse or groundwater resources could make an effective contribution to military action on account of their use, purpose or location. Water resources remain civilian objects and must be protected against direct attack and against excessive incidental damage.

It is also important to recall that, in order to qualify as a military objective, the contribution to military action must be both effective and make an effective contribution to military action of a party to the conflict. If an object merely contributes to the war effort, it does not qualify as a military objective. In addition, an attack must bring about a "definite military advantage", meaning that the advantage must be concrete and perceptible as opposed to merely hypothetical or speculative. Finally, the definite military advantage must be

110 Article 52 of the First Protocol. This definition is not included in the Second Protocol on non-international armed conflicts. However, other treaties applicable to civil wars include the definition of military objective. For a list of these treaties, see Jean-Marie Henckaerts & Louise Doswald-Beck (eds.), *Customary International Humanitarian Law, Vol. 1: Rules* (Cambridge University Press, 2005), pp. 26–29.

111 See the Declaration of the United Kingdom upon ratification of the First Protocol: "In relation to Article 52, that a specific area of land may be a military objective if, because of its location or other reasons specified in the Article, its total or partial destruction, capture or neutralization in the circumstances ruling at the time offers definite military advantage." (2 July 2002). See also the similar declarations of France, Italy, The Netherlands and Germany upon ratification of the First Protocol, https://ihl-databases.icrc.org/applic/ihl/ihl.nsf/States.xsp?xp_viewStates=XPages_NORMStatesParties&xp_treatySelected=615, last accessed on 15 October 2016.

offered "in the circumstances ruling at the time."[112] If the destruction of a given object does not yet offer, or no longer offers, a definite military advantage, the object does not constitute a military objective and must not be attacked.

It is also important to bear in mind that once an object has been identified as a military objective on the basis of the criteria laid out above, the attacker does not have unlimited licence to attack this object. Even if a military objective has been properly identified, an attack may still be prohibited under other rules of IHL, for example, if it would lead to excessive incidental damage to civilian objects and thus be contrary to the principle of proportionality. In addition, if the attack is intended, or may be expected, to cause widespread, long-term and severe damage to water resources, it is prohibited by Article 35.3 of the First Protocol even if it constitutes a military objective.

IV *Strengthening the Protection of Water Resources: International Criminal Law*

In addition to the rules of IHL, other bodies of international law contribute to and strengthen the protection of water resources during armed conflicts. The contribution of international criminal law through the Statute of the ICC (Part 1) and its practice (Part 2) is addressed below.

1 The Statute of the International Criminal Court

The First Protocol does not characterize the violation of the prohibition of causing widespread, long-lasting and serious damage to the natural environment as a grave breach. In 1998, however, the ICC Statute included environmental harm in its list of war crimes. According to Article 8.2 (b) (iv) of the Statute, the following amounts to a war crime:

> [i]ntentionally launching an attack in the knowledge that such attack will cause incidental loss of life or injury to civilians or damage to civilian objects or widespread, long-term and severe damage to the natural environment which would be clearly excessive in relation to the concrete and direct overall military advantage anticipated.[113]

The ICC Statute criminalizes the destruction of natural resources in similar terms to those found in the First Protocol: damage to the environment must be widespread, long-lasting and severe to trigger the Statute's application. Moreover, the Statute incorporates a proportionality requirement into its

112 Article 52.2 of the First Protocol.

113 Article 8.2 (b) (iv) of the ICC Statute.

definition of environmental harm as a war crime. Criminal responsibility is triggered if the damage caused was "widespread, long-lasting and severe" and this damage is "clearly excessive in relation to the concrete and direct overall military advantage anticipated."[114] An element that raises the bar of the First Protocol is the intentionality requirement: it must be proved that the attacker knew that his act would cause widespread, long-term and severe damage to the environment and that he intended to cause such damage.

It should be noted that Article 8.2 (b) (iv) of the ICC Statute is limited to international armed conflicts. Nevertheless, some of the Statute's provisions that do not directly deal with environmental protection provide a basis for criminalizing harm to the environment during non-international armed conflicts. Pursuant to Article 8.2 (c) of the ICC Statute, "serious violations of article 3 common to the four Geneva Conventions of 12 August 1949" are prohibited.[115] The term 'serious violations' encompasses a range of offences against individuals, like attacks on a person's life, physical integrity, and human dignity. It is possible that criminal responsibility could be incurred on the basis of attacks on a person's life and human dignity.[116] Making water resources unsafe for the population could by this means fall into the category of attacks on persons. Polluted water can certainly affect human health and living conditions.

Although the ICC Statute marks a significant development in the criminalization of environmental damage, international practice on this issue is still minimal. The challenges involved in establishing individual criminal responsibility for environmental offences were revealed in a report by the Committee of the ICTY Prosecutor. Referring to Article 8.2 (b) (iv) of the Statute "as an authoritative indicator for evolving customary international law",[117] the Committee decided not to recommend that the Prosecutor open an investigation.

2 The Arrest Warrant against President Omar Al Bashir

An interesting example of the issues raised by environmental protection is explored in Case Study 10 regarding the arrest warrant issued by the ICC's Pre-Trial Chamber against President Omar Al Bashir for war crimes, genocide and crimes against humanity. The warrant encompassed attacks intentionally

114 Ibid.

115 Article 8.2 (c) of the ICC Statute.

116 Carl Bruch, 'All's not Fair in (Civil) War: Criminal Liability of Environmental Damage in Internal Armed Conflict', *Vermont Law Review*, Vol. 25 (2001), p. 710.

117 Final Report to the Prosecutor by the Committee Established to Review the NATO Bombing Campaign against the Federal Republic of Yugoslavia (June 2000), paras. 15 and 21, http://www.icty.org/sid/10052, last accessed on 20 January 2016.

directed against a significant part of the population in Darfur, for acts of murder, extermination, rape, and torture, and the forcible displacement and looting of the property of a large number of civilians.

In 2008, the Security Council requested that the ICC Prosecutor investigate in Darfur, and on the basis of the evidence collected, the ICC Prosecutor, Luis Moreno-Ocampo concluded that there were reasonable grounds to believe that the President of Sudan, Omar Al Bashir, bore criminal responsibility for genocide, crimes against humanity and war crimes. This was the first arrest warrant of the ICC to be issued against an acting head of state. The majority of the Pre-Trial Chamber, with Judge Anita Ušacka dissenting, found that the evidence submitted in support of the Prosecution's application had not provided reasonable grounds for believing that the President had acted with a specific intention to destroy, in whole or in part, the Fur, Masalit and Zaghawa groups. The indictment's genocide charges do not therefore appear in the arrest warrant against President Omar Al Bashir.

It is notable that the Prosecutor stated that "[government] forces systematically destroyed the means of survival—including food, shelter, crops, livestock and, in particular, wells and water pumps—of the Fur, Masalit and Zaghawa populations in Darfur." Indeed, given the hostile desert environment and the lack of infrastructure, ensuring access to water is an essential component of populations' livelihoods needs. Many villagers dug common wells or maintained other common sources to meet the water needs of their communities and their cattle. The Janjaweed militias and the armed forces destroyed, polluted and poisoned these wells so as to deprive the villagers of water needed for survival.

The Prosecutor asked the Pre-Trial Chamber judges to recognize that damaging resources vital to the Darfur population constitutes one of the elements of genocide. The judges decided that "although there are reasonable grounds to believe that [government] forces at times contaminated the wells and water pumps of the towns and villages primarily inhabited by members of the Fur, Masalit and Zaghawa groups that they attacked, there are no reasonable grounds to believe that such a contamination was a core feature of their attacks." (para. 93).[118]

118 *Decision on the Prosecution's Application for a Warrant of Arrest against Omar Hassan Ahmad Al Bashir*, International Criminal Court, Pre-Trial Chamber, 4 March 2009, paras. 91–98 and 207, http://www.icc-cpi.int/iccdocs/doc/doc639096.pdf, last accessed on 20 January 2016.

The Pre-Trial Chamber's decision did not deny the relationship between depriving the population of access to water resources and the crime of genocide, but instead questioned the 'systematic' nature of the attacks by government forces. The decision did, however, leave the door open for the Prosecutor to submit additional evidence in order to amend the arrest warrant and include the crime of genocide. In addition, Judge Ušacka indicated in a dissenting opinion that the genocide charge "must be analysed in the context of Darfur's harsh terrain, in which water and food sources are naturally scarce, and shelter is of utmost importance." (para. 98). According to Judge Ušacka, the Chamber should have included the crime of genocide in its arrest warrant against President Al Bashir. She therefore seems to accept the Prosecutor's argument that environmental degradation depriving the population of essential means of survival may constitute an underlying element of the crime of genocide. In this way, this decision sets a significant precedent for environmental protection in times of armed conflict.

Case Study 10: Decision on the Prosecution's Application for a Warrant of Arrest against Omar Hassan Ahmad Al Bashir.

V *Conclusion*

During the conduct of hostilities, the protection of access to water is a fundamental objective of IHL. The rules of IHL confer on water the status of a civilian object to be protected from attack. This status must be understood in the context of the unique function of water with respect to other natural resources. Guaranteeing safe access to water ensures the survival of the population.

There are three fundamental pillars of water protection under IHL. The first addresses the protection of objects indispensable to the survival of the population and the prohibition on attacking works and installations containing dangerous forces. The second pillar includes the protection of the environment in times of armed conflict. The third pillar is based on the general principles of IHL.

The general principles of IHL may be used to set up a water protection framework. The Martens clause, which relies on the 'principles of humanity' and 'the dictates of public conscience', may serve to interpret the specific rules applicable to water and may be used to strengthen its protection through resort to norms of other areas of international law such as human rights law and international water law. The clause underlines the need to read the norms of IHL in conjunction with human rights law and international water law.

Other general principles such as the principles of proportionality and distinction also contribute to the protection of water. The principle of proportionality mandates that when an attack is launched against a legitimate military objective, the belligerents must assess whether this attack may cause indirect damage to water resources. In addition, the principle of distinction prevents indirect impacts. In the case of military operations carried out against industrial sites or electrical facilities, the parties to a conflict must determine if these objects qualify as military objectives under IHL and if these attacks "would be excessive in relation to the concrete and direct military advantage anticipated."[119] The determination must include the assessment of uncertain risks of indirect impacts on water resources caused by military operations.

Water may be used as a weapon or become a victim of war. IHL establishes a regulatory structure that can promote the protection of water but this regulatory structure has weaknesses. For example, water is not well protected against environmental damage. In addition, when the protection of water resources is understood as including related facilities like power plants that may be essential for the supply of drinking water, it becomes clear that the norms of IHL need consolidation and expansion. Power plant facilities are civilian objects that must be protected. These installations should be considered as "objects indispensable to the survival of the civilian population", protected in accordance with Article 54 of the First Protocol and Article 14 of the Second Protocol.[120] In some cases, electrical facilities are dual-use objects. In this context, before launching an attack, the parties to a conflict must assess whether electrical facilities provide essential water supplies to the civilian population. Even when these facilities are used for military purposes, the principles of proportionality and precaution must be applied.

B The Protection of Water under International Water Law

IHL is no longer the only branch of international law that ensures the protection of water resources and installations. Since the 1970s, international water law has paid attention to the link between the environment and armed conflict. Instruments regulating the uses, management and protection of water resources illustrate the development of international water law in this regard. Such instruments attend to international humanitarian concerns by protecting vital human needs. According to the commentaries to both

119 Article 57.2 (a) (iii) of the First Protocol.

120 Neither Article 54 of the First Protocol, nor Article 14 of the Second Protocol, contains an exhaustive list of indispensable objects. Sandoz; Swinarski & Zimmerman, supra, note 7, paras. 2103 and 4802.

the 1997 United Nations Convention on the Law of Non-Navigational Uses of International Watercourses ('UN Watercourses Convention') and the 2008 International Law Commission's Draft Articles on the Law of Transboundary Aquifers, riparian states are required to comply with norms of international humanitarian law applicable to international and non-international armed conflicts.[121] Furthermore, the 1997 UN Watercourses Convention seems to resolve the problem of some of its own provisions being impossible to perform in the wake of armed conflicts.[122]

In times of armed conflict, water resources are protected by the law of international watercourses. Given its specific characteristics, international water law establishes a regime protecting water resources as such or *'per se'*. While IHL protects water as a civilian object or as a part of the environment, international water law envisages the protection of water for its intrinsic value to the environment and human beings. In the context of international water law, the resolution adopted in 1976 by the International Law Association ('ILA') regarding the protection of water resources and water installations plays a crucial role in developing rules specifically dealing with armed conflicts in international water law, which take into account the negotiations of the Diplomatic Conference on the Reaffirmation and Development of International Humanitarian Law. Moreover, the *Institut de droit international* ('Institute of International Law' or 'IIL') and the International Law Commission ('ILC') have contributed to framing general principles regarding the application of treaties during armed conflicts (Part I).

The protection of water resources is ensured by international water law and international environmental law. For example, wetlands represent a particular ecosystem dependent on water resources that must be protected during armed conflicts. The 1972 Ramsar Convention on Wetlands of International Importance Especially as Waterfowl Habitat ('Ramsar Convention') plays a significant role in the protection of water resources both in times of peace and armed conflict (Part II).

The joint application of IHL and international water law has the potential to enhance the protection of water resources during armed conflicts. The observance of international watercourse treaties avoids the risk of serious damage to other watercourse states. As the ICJ has recalled, states must "ensure that activities within their jurisdiction and control respect the environment of

121 Article 29 of the UN Watercourses Convention and Article 18 of the ILC Draft Articles on Transboundary Aquifers.

122 See, for example, Article 30 of the UN Watercourses Convention.

other States."[123] The application of international watercourse treaties plays a key role in the implementation of this general obligation (Part III).

I *Water Treaties and Armed Conflicts*

This section will examine the general framework for understanding the effects of armed conflicts on international watercourse regimes by looking at some instruments developed by the ILA since the 1970s (Part 1) and the general principles applicable to the effects of armed conflicts on treaties embodied in the Draft Articles on the Effects of Armed Conflicts on Treaties adopted by the International Law Commission in 2011 (Part 2).

1 The Role of the International Law Association (ILA) in the Development of Principles on the Protection of Water Resources in Times of Armed Conflict

There are few international instruments that expressly deal with the protection of water resources and water installations in times of armed conflict. The work of the ILA has significantly contributed to the development of a specific set of rules on the protection of water resources during armed conflicts.

The Helsinki Rules on the Uses of the Waters of International Rivers ('Helsinki Rules'), adopted by the ILA at its Helsinki Conference in 1966, contain only one article (Article XX), which refers to problems arising from armed conflicts, and it is confined to the limited subject of navigation. Aware of the *lacuna* in the legal protection of water in wartime, the ILA addressed the issue again ten years later. In 1976, during its fifty-seventh Conference held at Madrid, the ILA adopted a resolution on the protection of water resources and water installations in wartime.[124] In 2004, the Berlin Rules on Water Resources also affirmed the protection of water in times of armed conflicts, following the same approach taken by the 1976 Resolution.

The Helsinki Rules constitute one of the first texts adopted at the universal level that sets out general principles and obligations on the uses, management and protection of international watercourses. According to the 1966 Helsinki Rules, in times of armed conflict or when a public emergency threatens the life of a state, a riparian state may take measures derogating from freedom of navigation to the extent strictly required by the exigencies of the situation and

123 ICJ, *Legality of the Threat or Use of Nuclear Weapons, Advisory Opinion, I.C.J. Reports 1996*, p. 226, at p. 242, para. 29.

124 'Protection of Water Resources and Water Installations in Times of Armed Conflict. Report of the Fifty-Seven Conference', *International Law Association* (1976), pp. 213–266, p. xxxiv.

provided that the measures are not contrary to other obligations under international law. These obligations include the rules of IHL. Where a party to a conflict derogates from the freedom of navigation, the concerned state must reconcile the obligations imposed by the principle of free navigation with humanitarian purposes.[125] The Helsinki Rules underline the fundamental role that watercourses may play in the transportation of the wounded and the sick during armed conflicts. A riparian state cannot take measures to impede the navigation of military hospital ships or private vessels used to "assist, treat and transport wounded, sick and shipwrecked" persons.[126] According to Article 23 of the 1977 First Protocol, "[m]edical ships and craft shall, whether at sea or in other waters, be respected and protected."[127] These ships may not be attacked. Some authors have insisted on the value of this provision with respect to navigation on international watercourses or lakes, stating that "[f]or the first time in any of the conventions on the law of war, there is a reference not only to 'at sea' but also to 'or other waters'. By including this additional phrase the 1977 Diplomatic Conference added warfare on inland waters and lakes to the ambit of this article."[128] Ships and other craft may transport the wounded, the sick or medical supplies on inland waters such as rivers, canals or lakes. In those cases, the free navigation of these ships must be protected.[129]

The 1966 Helsinki Rules only affirm the principle of freedom of navigation for humanitarian purposes during armed conflicts. The ILA Resolution adopted in Madrid in 1976 ensures a broader protection of water resources during armed conflicts.[130] In its preliminary report, drafted in 1974, the ILA's Committee on International Water Resources affirmed that:

> It is only in the last decade that the new awareness of the world-wide threat to human environment has meant a turning point also in the

125 Article XX states that: "In times of war, other armed conflict, or public emergency constituting a threat to the life of the State, a riparian State may take measures derogating from its obligations under this Chapter to the extent strictly required by the exigencies of the situation, provided that such measures are inconsistent with its other obligations under international law. The riparian State shall in any case facilitate navigation for humanitarian purpose."

126 Sandoz; Swinarski & Zimmerman, supra, note 9, p. 156.

127 Article 23 of the 1977 First Protocol.

128 Howard S. Levie, *The Code of International Armed Conflict*, Vol. 2, (Oceana Publications, 1986), p. 534.

129 Sandoz; Swinarski & Zimmerman, supra, note 9, pp. 267–268.

130 'Protection of Water Resources and Water Installations in Times of Armed Conflict. Report of the Fifty-Seven Conference', supra, note 124, pp. 213–266.

> considerations concerning the protection of water and water installations in times of armed conflict, although these considerations are still far from being materially comprehensive or methodically systematic. The dangers menacing dams and consequently the civil population living in the potential flood area of such dams have been visualized by a number of Governments and have led to municipal legislation providing for special protection, notably in Switzerland, Sweden and Germany.[131]

A key aspect of the 1976 Madrid Resolution is its contribution to the strengthening of the norms of IHL in the area of the protection of water resources and water installations. The preamble of the Resolution underlines "the urgent need to establish precise rules for the protection of water and water installations against damage or destruction and thus to contribute to the development of international humanitarian law applicable to armed conflicts."[132]

In its work, the ILA takes into account the work of the 1974–1977 Diplomatic Conference on the Reaffirmation and Development of International Humanitarian Law. The Project of the First Protocol adopted in 1975 is explicitly mentioned in the ILA Resolution.[133] Several Articles of the 1976 ILA Resolution affirm the same rules as those contained in the First Protocol, like the protection of the objects indispensable to the survival of the population and the protection of installations such as dams and dykes.[134] Moreover, the Resolution reaffirms the prohibition on using poison contained in the 1907 Hague Regulations.[135] In this context, it states that "[w]ater which is indispensable for the health and survival of the civilian population should not be poisoned or rendered otherwise unfit for human consumption."[136]

The Resolution also regulates several aspects related to the 'weaponization' of water. It contains specific articles on the diversion of water resources, the causing of floods and other uses of water which may "[interfere] with

131 *Yearbook of the International Law Commission*, vol. II, Part One (1982), p. 167.

132 Ibid.

133 Eero J. Manner & Veli-Martti Metsalampi, *The Work of the ILA on the Law of International Water Resources* (1976), pp. 128–129.

134 Article 2 of the ILA Resolution reads: "Water supply installations which are indispensable for the minimum conditions of survival of the civilian population should not be cut off or destroyed."

135 Article 23 of the 1907 Hague Regulations forbids: "to employ poison or poisoned weapons." Convention IV Respecting the Laws and Customs of War on Land, The Hague, 18 October 1907.

136 Article I of the 1976 Resolution.

the hydrological balance."[137] These provisions are innovative and original with respect to the protection of water during armed conflicts. In particular, Article III of the 1976 Resolution reads:

> The diversion of waters for military purposes should be prohibited when it would cause disproportionate suffering to the civilian population or substantial damage to the ecological balance of the area concerned. A diversion that is carried out in order to damage or destroy the minimum conditions of survival of the civilian population or the basic ecological balance of the area concerned or in order to terrorize the population should be prohibited in any case.[138]

The diversion of waters is prohibited when it would cause disproportionate suffering to the population. In this way, the Resolution takes into account the proportionality between the military advantage and the deprivation of water suffered by the population. Another element that the Resolution takes into consideration is the environmental impact of the watercourse diversion. Article III provides that the diversion of waters for military purposes should be prohibited when it causes "substantial damage to the ecological balance of the area concerned." The use of the adjective 'substantial' points to a threshold, which is less high than the threshold of Articles 35.3 and 55 of the 1977 First Protocol. The ILA Resolution therefore recognizes the sensitive character of water resources and aquatic ecosystems. The diversion of waters may negatively affect this fragile ecosystem.

The ILA Resolution of 1976 envisages another situation in which water can be used as a weapon. It is prohibited to use "floods as well as any other interference with the hydrological balance" as a means or method of war. This provision prohibits any use of water for military purposes if this "involves grave dangers to the civilian population."[139] This rule underlines the relationship between the use of water as a weapon of war and its impact on the population.

The ILA Resolution is a thorough document regulating the protection of water in time of armed conflict. The Resolution provides rules on the duties and obligations of the occupant, on the uses of water resources, and on the effect of armed conflicts on water treaties.[140] It also specifies that a peace

137 Article V of the 1976 Resolution.

138 Article III of the 1976 Resolution.

139 Article V of the 1976 Resolution.

140 Article VII states that: "The effect of the outbreak of war on the validity of treaties or of parts thereof concerning the use of water resources should not be termination but

treaty must not deprive a people of its water resources. When, as a result of the drawing of a new frontier, a hydraulic system in the territory of one state is dependent on installations located in the territory of another state, the delivery of water supplies indispensable to the vital needs of the people must be ensured.[141] As can be seen, the 1976 Resolution establishes a broad protection of water during armed conflicts.

In 2004, the ILA adopted the Berlin Rules on water resources, revising the 1966 Helsinki Rules. Since 1966, there have been many developments in international law regarding water resources. The UN Convention on the Law of the Non-Navigational Uses of International Watercourses established a certain number of principles on the uses, protection and management of transboundary water resources. Moreover, IHL and human rights law have developed specific norms on the protection of water resources and water installations. These developments were underlined in the 2004 Berlin Rules, which stated that:

> Today, the situation is significantly different than in 1966. [...] The emergence of a body of international law addressing significant environmental problems and the protection of basic human rights since 1966 has broadened and deepened the role of customary international law applicable to the world's waters.[142]

Therefore, the Berlin Rules

> incorporate the experience of the nearly four decades since the Helsinki Rules were adopted, taking into account the development of important bodies of international environmental law, international human rights law, and the humanitarian law relating to the war and armed conflict, as

---

only suspension. Such suspension should take place only when the purpose of the war or military necessity imperatively demand the suspension and when the minimum requirements of subsistence for the civil population are safeguarded."

141 Article VIII provides that: "1. It should be prohibited to deprive, by the provisions of a peace treaty or similar instrument, a people of its water resources to such an extent that a threat to the health or to the economic or physical conditions of survival is created. 2. When, as the result of the fixing of a new frontier, the hydraulic system in the territory of one State is dependent on works established in the territory of another State, arrangements should be made for the safeguarding of uninterrupted delivery of water supplies indispensable for the vital needs of the people."

142 'Final Report on the Berlin Rules on Water Resources', *International Law Association* (2004), p. 3, http://internationalwaterlaw.org/documents/intldocs/ILA_Berlin_Rules-2004.pdf, last accessed on 20 January 2016.

well as the adoption by the General Assembly of the United Nations of the UN Convention.[143]

The Articles of the 2004 Berlin Rules are based on the 1976 ILA Resolution and the 1977 First and Second Protocols.[144] For example, the principle that prohibits poisoning or otherwise rendering unfit for human consumption water that is indispensable to the health and survival of the population is now recognized as a clear obligation of the parties to a conflict.[145] Moreover, the prohibition on attacking installations indispensable to the survival of the population is inspired by the 1977 Protocols. The approach taken by the Berlin Rules regarding the protection of the environment, however, seems conservative. According to the Berlin Rules, the belligerents cannot destroy or divert waters when "such acts would cause widespread, long-term, and severe ecological damage prejudicial to the health or survival of the population."[146] In this case, a better approach would have been to limit the damage to "acts [that] would fundamentally impair the ecological integrity of waters", based on the 1976 Madrid Resolution that fixes a lower threshold of harm to trigger environmental protection norms.

The ILA has accomplished significant and innovative work on the protection of water during and after armed conflicts. The prohibitions against diverting rivers,[147] causing floods[148] and impairing ecological integrity of waters[149] are original contributions to the protection of transboundary water resources. Moreover, the 1976 Madrid Resolution states that, after an armed conflict, peace agreements should not deprive a population of its essential resources.[150]

143 Ibid., p. 4.

144 See Chapter X, Articles 50–55 of the 2004 Berlin Rules.

145 Compare Article 50 of the Berlin Rules and Article I of the 1976 Resolution.

146 Article 52 of the Berlin Rules.

147 Article III of the 1976 Madrid Resolution and Article 51 of the Berlin Rules.

148 Article V of the 1976 Madrid Resolution states that "The causing of floods as well as any other interference with the hydrological balance [...] should be prohibited when it involves grave dangers to the civilian population or substantial damage to the ecological balance of the area concerned".

149 Article 52 of the Berlin Rules.

150 Article VIII of the Madrid Resolution affirms that: "It should be prohibited to deprive, by the provisions of a peace treaty or similar instrument, a people of its water resources to such an extent that a threat to the health or to the economic or physical conditions is created. When as a result of the fixing of a new frontier, the hydraulic system in the territory of one State is dependent on works established in the territory of another, arrangements

This recognition plays an important role in the protection of the rights of communities after an armed conflict.

2 General Principles Applicable to the Effects of Armed Conflicts on Treaties: The Role of the Institute of International Law (IIL) and the International Law Commission (ILC)

The Institute of International Law began to work at a very early stage on the effects of armed conflicts on treaties. The Regulations regarding the effects of war on treaties (*"Règlement concernant les effets de la guerre sur les traités"*) adopted by the IIL at its 1912 Christiania session provide that war does not jeopardize "the existence of treaties, conventions and agreements, regardless of their title and object."[151] In the second half of the twentieth century, during its 1985 Helsinki session, the Institute adopted a resolution on the effects of armed conflicts on treaties. This resolution asserts the principle that the outbreak of an armed conflict does not *ipso facto* entail the termination of the treaties in force between the parties to the armed conflict or the suspension of their application.[152] This principle, which is key to understanding the effects of armed conflicts on treaties, was incorporated by the ILC into its 2011 Draft Articles on the Effects of Armed Conflicts on Treaties.[153]

In its Draft Articles, the ILC sets out general criteria to delineate the impact of armed conflicts on treaty instruments. According to the ILC, in order to determine whether a treaty continues to apply during a period of armed conflict or if it can potentially be terminated, suspended or subject to withdrawal, states should consider general criteria such as the extent, scale and duration of the armed conflict.[154] The Commission chose not to identify the specific

should be made for the safeguarding of uninterrupted delivery of water supplies indispensable for the vital needs of the people."

151 *Yearbook of the IIL* (1912), p. 611.

152 Article 2, *Yearbook of the IIL* (1992), p. 174.

153 Article 3 of the Draft Articles on the Effects of Armed Conflicts on Treaties provides that: "The existence of an armed conflict does not *ipso facto* terminate or suspend the operation of treaties: (a) as between States parties to the conflict; (b) as between a State party to the conflict and a State that is not." 'Draft Articles on the Effects of Armed Conflicts on Treaties', *Yearbook of the International Law Commission*, vol. II, Part Two (2011).

154 Article 5 of the Draft Articles affirms that: "The rules of international law on treaty interpretation shall be applied to establish whether a treaty is susceptible to termination, withdrawal or suspension in the event of an armed conflict." Article 6 states that "In order to ascertain whether a treaty is susceptible to termination, withdrawal or suspension in the event of an armed conflict, regard shall be had to all relevant factors, including: a) the

treaties that would continue to operate. Instead, it developed an indicative list of treaties "the subject matter of which involves an implication that they continue in operation, in whole or in part, during armed conflict." This list includes "treaties relating to international watercourses and related installations and facilities", "treaties relating to aquifers and related installations and facilities" as well as "treaties relating to the international protection of the environment."[155] This finding of the ILC makes clear that treaties on international watercourses, aquifers and related installations are not automatically terminated or suspended during an armed conflict. States that are parties to a conflict continue to be bound by the rights and obligations created by water treaties.

This being said, we should examine the different ways in which bodies of rules interact. The accepted analytical method when confronted with interacting rules is to apply the *lex specialis*.[156] When two rules govern the same situation, in theory, this principle gives precedence to the rules governing the more specific subject matter. In this case, this means applying international humanitarian law and setting aside other areas of international law such as international environmental law and international water law. It should be noted, however, that the international case law has, while invoking this principle, favoured a systemic approach to the relationship between different applicable bodies of law, particularly in the case of the relationship between IHL and human rights. As discussed in Case Study 11, the International Court of Justice's Advisory Opinion on the *Legal Consequences of the Construction of a Wall in the Occupied Palestinian Territory* and its Judgment in *Armed Activities on the Territory of the Congo* are illustrative.

nature of the treaty, in particular its subject-matter, its object and purpose, its content and the number of parties to the treaty; and (b) the characteristics of the armed conflict, such as its territorial extent, its scale and intensity, its duration and, in the case of non-international armed conflict, also the degree of outside involvement." Ibid.

155 Article 7 provides that: "An indicative list of treaties the subject-matter of which involves an implication that they continue in operation, in whole or in part, during armed conflict, is to be found in the annex to the present draft Articles." Ibid.

156 See Cordula Droege, 'Elective Affinities? Human Rights and Humanitarian Law', *International Review of the Red Cross*, Vol. 90 (871) (2008), pp. 507–509; Marco Sassòli, 'Le droit international humanitaire, une "lex specialis" par rapport aux droits humains?', *in*, Andreas Auer; Alexander Fluckiger & Michel Hottelier (eds.), *Les droits de l'homme et la Constitution: études en l'honneur du Professeur Giorgio Malinverni* (Schuttless, 2007), pp. 376–377.

In its Advisory Opinion on the *Legal Consequences of the Construction of a Wall in the Occupied Palestinian Territory*, although the Court reiterated that the principle of *lex specialis* governs the relationship between humanitarian law and human rights law, it also concluded that in this case, the construction of the wall violated provisions from both bodies of law at the same time.[157] It has been observed that the Court's opinion "[makes] clear that *lex specialis* is not being used to displace [human rights law, but that it] is rather an indication that human rights bodies should interpret a human rights norm in light of [humanitarian law]."[158]

Moreover, in its Judgment in *Armed Activities on the Territory of the Congo*,[159] the Court's approach clearly promoted a consistent interpretation of both IHL and human rights law in order to foster systemic integration. In that decision, the Court confirmed that IHL and international human rights law continue to be applicable in times of armed conflict, asserting that Uganda had the duty, as an occupying force, to monitor compliance with international legal norms relating to human rights and humanitarian law.

Case Study 11: The Advisory Opinion on the *Legal Consequences of the Construction of a Wall in the Occupied Palestinian Territory* and the Judgment in *Armed Activities on the Territory of the Congo.*

It would no doubt be appropriate to adopt a similar understanding of the relationship between humanitarian law and other areas of international law like international water law and international environmental law in order to advance a systemic approach to these branches of international law. One of the key methods of this approach derives from the principle of systemic integration, based on Article 31 (3) (c) of the Vienna Convention on the Law of Treaties. Pursuant to this Article, treaty interpretation should take into account "[a]ny relevant rules of international law applicable in the relations between the parties."[160] This provision places the relationship between norms from different bodies of law in the context of the rules of treaty interpretation.

157 ICJ, *Legal Consequences of the Construction of a Wall in the Occupied Palestinian Territory, Advisory Opinion, I.C.J. Reports 2004*, p. 136, at para. 55.

158 Françoise Hampson & Ibrahim Salama, *Working paper on the relationship between human rights law and international humanitarian law*, UN Doc. E/CN.4/Sub.2/2005/14 (21 June 2005), para. 57.

159 ICJ, *Armed Activities on the Territory of the Congo (Democratic Republic of the Congo* v. *Uganda), Judgment, I.C.J. Reports 2005*, p. 168, at para. 178.

160 Article 31 (3) (c) of the Vienna Convention on the Law of Treaties.

It expresses the principle of systemic integration, according to which treaties must be interpreted in light of the relevant rules and principles of international law applicable in the relations between the parties. This principle allows us to examine the relationship between different bodies of law. It offers a method of interpretation for resolving conflicts arising from the overlap between different international legal rules in a manner that ensures their consistency with general international law.[161]

II *International Environmental Law and the Protection of Water*

The ecosystems of water resources are protected by instruments of international environmental law. This section will look at some principles related to the continued applicability of these instruments (Part 1) and then will consider the role of Multilateral Environmental Agreements ('MEAS') and UNEP to the protection of water resources during armed conflicts (Part 2). Finally, the monograph will examine the complementary role of customary international law principles in the protection of water resources during armed conflicts (Part 3).

1 The Applicability of Instruments Protecting the Environment to Water Resources

The ICJ's Advisory Opinion on the *Legality of the Threat or Use of Nuclear Weapons* recognized that "the environment is not an abstraction but represents the living space" of human beings.[162] The ICJ Advisory Opinion was an important step towards recognizing the great significance and concrete importance of the environment. Furthermore, despite the ICJ determining that the objective of its advisory opinion was not to declare "whether the treaties relating to the protection of the environment are or not applicable during an armed conflict", some states in their oral and written statements supported the notion of the continued relevance of environmental treaties during armed conflicts.[163] The continued applicability of environmental treaties after the outbreak of

161 It has been observed: "This is all that Article 31 (3) (c) requires; the integration into the process of legal reasoning—including reasoning by courts and tribunals—of a sense of coherence and meaningfulness." 'Fragmentation of international law: Difficulties arising from the diversification and expansion of international law', *Study Group of the International Law Commission*, A/CN.4/L.682 (2006), para. 419.

162 ICJ, *Legality of the Threat or Use of Nuclear Weapons, Advisory Opinion, I.C.J. Reports 1996*, p. 226, para. 29.

163 Momtaz, supra, note 57, p. 360. See also Karine Mollard-Bannelier, *La protection de l'environnement en temps de conflit armé* (Pedone, 2001), pp. 266–279.

war is in many cases of vital importance for the protection of water resources and even for the health and survival of the population, especially when these treaties deal with the protection of drinking and irrigation water or ensure measures of flood control.

Some instruments of international environmental law include general principles relating to armed conflict without however specifically addressing whether they continue to apply during armed conflicts. Such is the case of the 1972 Stockholm Declaration on the Human Environment and the 1982 World Charter for Nature. The latter affirms the "general principles" that "nature shall be secured against degradation caused by warfare or other hostile activities" and that "military activities damaging to nature shall be avoided."[164]

The Rio Declaration on the Environment and Development provides something of an answer: "States shall [...] respect international law providing protection for the environment in times of armed conflict." The Declaration does not, however, discuss the applicability of environmental protection treaties during armed conflicts.[165] A clear-cut answer on the topic is provided by the ICRC 'Guidelines for Military Manuals and Instructions on the Protection of the Environment in Times of Armed Conflict'. According to this document, "[i]nternational environmental agreements and relevant rules of customary law may continue to be applicable in times of armed conflict to the extent that they are not inconsistent with the applicable law of armed conflict."[166]

In a 1994 Resolution, the UN General Assembly referred to the ICRC Guidelines on the protection of the environment. It recommended that states "disseminate these rules [...] as widely as possible" and "include them in their programmes of military and civil instruction."[167] The General Assembly reit-

164 World Charter for Nature, A/RES/37/7 (1982), paras. 5 and 20. See also Principle 26 of the Stockholm Declaration, affirming that "Man and his environment must be spared the effects of nuclear weapons and all other means of mass destruction. States must strive to reach prompt agreement, in the relevant international organs, on the elimination and complete destruction of such weapons." Stockholm Declaration, supra, note 40.

165 Principle 24 declares that: "Warfare is inherently destructive of sustainable development. States shall therefore respect international law providing protection for the environment in times of armed conflict and cooperate in its further development, as necessary." Available at: http://www.unep.org/documents.multilingual/default.asp?documentid=78&articleid=1163, last accessed on 20 January 2016.

166 'Guidelines for Military Manuals and Instructions on the Protection of the Environment in Times of Armed Conflict', Article 5. Resolution A/RES/49/50 (1994), https://www.icrc.org/eng/resources/documents/article/other/57jn38.htm, last accessed on 15 October 2016.

167 Resolution A/RES/49/50 (9 December 1994), para. 11.

erated this invitation in a 1996 Resolution.[168] The Guidelines therefore affirm the continued applicability of instruments of international environmental law in times of armed conflict, even if their implementation depends on their integration into military manuals.[169] The Resolution adopted by the General Assembly of UNEP ('UNEA Resolution') in 2016 further stresses this obligation and states "the importance of the implementation by all Member States of international law applicable to the protection of the environment in areas affected by armed conflict in line with Member States' legal responsibilities".[170] This Resolution could constitute an entry point to the adoption of a specific instrument on the protection of natural resources during armed conflicts.

Most environmental treaties are silent on the issue of their applicability following the outbreak of military hostilities. There are, however, some treaties that pay attention to the impact of armed conflict on their operation. For example, conventions on civil liability for damage include provisions excluding their applicability when damage occurs as a result of war and armed conflict.[171] Others include provisions permitting their total or partial suspension at the instigation of one its parties, if that party is engaged in a conflict.[172] Some treaties also require that treaty bodies take into account the consequences of

168 Resolution A/RES/51/157 (30 January 1997), para. 19.

169 Silja Vöneky, 'A New Shield for the Environment: Peacetime Treaties as Legal Restraints of Wartime Damage', *Review of European, Comparative & International Environmental Law* (*RECIEL*), Vol. 9(1) (2000), pp. 20–32, at p. 22.

170 United Nations Environment Assembly (UNEA) Resolution, UNEP/EA.2/ L.16/REV.1 (May 2016).

171 See, for example, Article 9 of the 1960 Paris Convention on Third-Party Liability in the Field of Nuclear Energy (29 July 1960, as amended by the Additional Protocol of 28 January 1964 and by the Protocol of 16 November 1982); Article IV (3) (a) of the 1963 Vienna Convention on Civil Liability for Nuclear Damage (21 May 1963); Article 4 (5) (a) of the 1999 Protocol on Liability and Compensation for Damage Resulting from Transboundary Movements of Hazardous Wastes and their Disposal (10 December 1999); Article 4 (2) (a) of the 2003 Protocol on Civil Liability and Compensation for Damage Caused by the Transboundary Effects of Industrial Accidents on Transboundary Waters to the 1992 Convention on the Protection and Use of Transboundary Watercourses and International Lakes and to the 1992 Convention on the Transboundary Effects of Industrial Accidents (21 May 2003).

172 Article XIX (1) of the International Convention for the Prevention of Pollution of the Sea by Oil (12 May 1954). The Convention allows "parties to suspend operation of whole or part of the Convention in case of war or other hostilities if they consider themselves affected as a belligerent or as a neutral upon notification to the Convention's Bureau."

hostilities in applying the treaty.[173] Furthermore, one treaty leaves open, for example, the possibility of states parties deciding to apply a convention to its warships and other vessels, as long as the Secretary General is notified of the decision.[174]

Instruments dealing with water resources have adopted a specific approach to the issue of their applicability in times of armed conflict. This specificity is based on the fact that these instruments reiterate that IHL norms are applicable during armed conflicts. Thus, Article 29 of the 1997 UN Watercourses Convention and Article 18 of the ILC Draft Articles on Transboundary Aquifers affirm in similar terms that transboundary water resources and related works and installations "shall enjoy the protection accorded by the principles and rules of international law applicable in international and non-international armed conflicts and shall not be used in violation of these principles and rules".[175] The 2000 Revised Protocol on Shared Watercourses of the Southern African Development Community ('SADC')[176] contains similar language. The application of both IHL and international water law contribute to strengthening the protection of water resources. In particular, fresh water agreements impose specific obligations on riparian states. For example, the prohibition not to cause significant harm embodied in Article 7 of the UN Watercourses Convention sets out a lower threshold as compared to Articles 35.3 and 55 of the 1977 First Protocol, which prohibit "widespread, long-term and severe damage" to the environment.

2 Multilateral Environmental Agreements (MEAs) and Water

International environmental law contributes in a variety of ways to the protection of water resources. There has been a growing awareness of the connections between water and the environment. Principles and norms of international environmental law have emerged and are incorporated in many treaties dealing with

173 Article IV (2) of the International Convention for the High Seas Fisheries of the North Pacific Ocean (9 May 1952).

174 Article 4 (5) of the 1996 International Convention on Liability and Compensation for Damage in Connection with the Carriage of Hazardous and Noxious Substances by Sea (3 May 1996).

175 Article 18.

176 Article 4 (3) (c) (iii) provides that: "Shared watercourses and related installations, facilities, and other works shall enjoy the protection accorded by the principles and rules of the law applicable in international and non-international armed conflict and shall not be used in violation of those principles and rules". Revised Protocol on Shared Watercourses (7 August 2000).

transboundary water resources. A number of MEAs are concerned with the protection of these resources and their institutional mechanisms are dedicated to the implementation of these agreements. Instruments of international environmental law and those focused on fresh water complement each other in enhancing the protection and management of fresh water.[177] Water resources are protected by MEAs aiming at the protection of the environment such as the 1971 Ramsar Convention,[178] the 1992 Convention on Biological Diversity,[179] the 1972 Convention concerning the Protection of the World Cultural and Natural Heritage ('UNESCO World Heritage Convention')[180] or the 1989 Basel Convention on the Control of Transboundary Movements of Hazardous Wastes and their Disposal ('Basel Convention').[181]

The Basel Convention, for example, establishes a specific notification procedure for transboundary movements of hazardous wastes. This procedure contributes to the prevention of environmental damage.[182] In a 2005 Resolution on the Permanent Sovereignty of the Palestinian People in the Occupied Palestinian Territory, the UN General Assembly pointed out that the occupying power, must cease

> the dumping of all kinds of waste materials in the Occupied Palestinian Territory, including East Jerusalem, and in the occupied Syrian Golan, which gravely threaten their natural resources, namely the water and

177 Laurence Boisson de Chazournes, *Fresh Water in International Law* (Oxford University Press, 2013), p. 109.

178 Convention on Wetlands of International Importance Especially as Waterfowl Habitat (2 February 1971).

179 Convention on Biological Diversity (5 June 1992).

180 Convention concerning the Protection of the World Cultural and Natural Heritage (16 November 1972).

181 Convention on the Control of Transboundary Movements of Hazardous Wastes and their Disposal (22 March 1989).

182 Article 6 provides that the state of export shall require the generator or exporter to notify, in writing, the competent authority of the states concerned of any proposed transboundary movement of hazardous wastes or other waste. Moreover, the state of export "shall not allow the generator or exporter to commence the transboundary movement until it has received written confirmation that (a) the notifier has received the written consent of the State of import; and (b) The notifier has received from the State of import confirmation of the existence of a contract between the exporter and the disposer specifying environmentally sound management of the wastes in question." Ibid.

> land resources, and pose an environmental hazard and health threat to the civilian populations.[183]

Waste management may affect water resources, especially groundwater resources. This impact may be particularly negative in arid regions such as Israel and Palestine. In this context, the implementation of the Basel Convention's notification obligations is of particular importance in preventing environmental damage.

The damming and deviation of international rivers can endanger wetland ecosystems. A case in point is the environmental degradation of the Mesopotamian marshes between Iran and Iraq, which form part of the Tigris and Euphrates basins. During the 1950s, dams built by Turkey and Syria triggered the desiccation of the marshes. The impact of upstream damming and Saddam Hussein's massive drainage works during the late 1980s had devastating impacts on this unique ecosystem. Since 2000, the evaluation impact studies conducted by UNEP on the reduction of the Mesopotamian marshes have compared it to the drying up of the Aral Sea and the deforestation of the Amazon.[184] In 2004, thanks to a UNEP-led mediation, representatives of Iran and Iraq met for the first time in order to establish a common approach to the protection of the Mesopotamian marshes. Following the meeting, the parties decided to exchange data and information on transboundary water issues.[185]

In its 2001 and 2007 reports, UNEP recommended the participation of Iraq in the Ramsar Convention, and it further recommended the inclusion of the Mesopotamian marshlands in the List of Wetlands of International Importance established by the Convention. After participating in 2005 as an observer at the Conference of Parties of the Ramsar Convention, Iraq acceded to the Convention. The first wetland of international importance registered by Iraq was Hawizeh, a wetland that is part of the Mesopotamian marshes.[186] In addition, UNEP recommended the establishment of an international agreement on the Tigris and Euphrates among all riparian countries to sustainably

183 Resolution 60/183 (22 December 2005), para. 7.

184 'Natural and Cultural Management of the Iraqi Marshlands', UNEP-UNESCO Joint Project, http://www.unep.or.jp/ietc/IraqWH/index.html, last accessed on 20 January 2016.

185 'Desk Study on the Situation of the Environment in Iraq', supra, note 64, p. 39.

186 Profile of the country, http://www.ramsar.org/wetland/iraq, last accessed on 17 January 2016.

manage these shared waters.[187] Since 2009, UNESCO and UNEP have collaborated to include the Mesopotamian marshes in the World Heritage List.[188]

Another informative case regarding the role of UNEP related to armed conflicts concerns the Sistan wetlands shared between Iran and Afghanistan. At the beginning of the 2000s, tensions between the two countries escalated because of water scarcity in the basin. In 2002, UNEP undertook an evaluation assessment on the Helmand River basin in Afghanistan, including the Sistan wetlands. The need for better transboundary water cooperation was one of the main recommendations of UNEP. Following this assessment, both countries asked UNEP to generate additional scientific information and provide environmental diplomacy support to the parties. Thus, a technical meeting was hosted in Geneva. During the meeting, the results from a satellite survey on the environmental conditions of the Sistan wetlands were shared between Afghanistan and Iran and the countries agreed to develop a joint proposal for international funding to restore the wetlands.[189]

3 The Protection Offered by International Customary Law

In its Advisory Opinion on the *Legality of the Threat or Use of Nuclear Weapons*, the ICJ emphasized that states have the obligation to protect the environment during armed conflict. The Court underlined that states must take into account environmental considerations when assessing what is necessary and proportionate in pursuit of military goals.[190] This duty arises from the general prohibition not to cause damage to the environment of other states. According

---

187 UNEP, *The Mesopotamian Marshlands. Demise of an Ecosystem* (2001), p. 35, http://eoimages.gsfc.nasa.gov/images/imagerecords/1000/1716/meso2.pdf, last accessed on 20 January 2016. For an analysis of the Tigris and Euphrates water basins, see Julien Cazala, 'Le droit international de l'eau et les différends relatifs au Tigre et à l'Euphrate', *in*, Laurence Boisson de Chazournes & Salman M.A. Salman (eds.), *Water Resources and International Law, The Hague Academy of International Law* (Brill, 2004), pp. 533–575.

188 On the role of multilateral environmental agreements in armed conflict, see Britta Sjöstedt, 'The Role of Multilateral Environmental Agreements in Armed Conflict: "Green-keeping" in Virunga Park. Applying the UNESCO World Heritage Convention in the Armed Conflict of the Democratic Republic of Congo', *Nordic Journal of International Law*, Vol. 82 (2013), pp. 129–153.

189 'Natural Resources and Conflict. A Guide for Mediation Practitioners', UNEP/UNDPA (2015), pp. 76–77, http://postconflict.unep.ch/publications/UNDPA_UNEP_NRC_Mediation_full.pdf, last accessed on 15 October 2016.

190 ICJ, *Legality of the Threat or Use of Nuclear Weapons, Advisory Opinion, I.C.J. Reports 1996*, p. 226, at p. 242, para. 30.

to Principle 21 of the Declaration adopted at the Stockholm Conference in 1972 and Principle 2 of the Declaration on Environment and Development adopted at the Rio Conference in 1992, states have "[t]he duty to ensure that activities within their jurisdiction or control do not cause damage to the environment of other States or of areas beyond the limits of national jurisdiction."[191]

The Stockholm Declaration and the Rio Declaration emphasize that the prohibition against causing damage to the environment applies regarding a state's activities both in its national territory and in the territories of other states. When a state exercises 'control' outside its national territory, it must ensure that its military operations do not cause environmental damage. In occupied territories subject to 'de facto' control, the occupying power is bound by this obligation. This principle was emphasized by the ICJ in its Advisory Opinion on the *Legality of the Threat or Use of Nuclear Weapons*, by stating: "the general obligation of States to ensure that activities within their jurisdiction and control respect the environment of other States or of areas beyond national control is now part of the corpus of international law relating to the environment."[192] The Court recognized that this principle has a customary nature and is applicable in times of armed conflict. This obligation also applies to activities carried out beyond national territory, i.e. in the territories 'under the control' of a party to a conflict.

Customary obligations to protect the environment in times of armed conflict include the general obligation of states to respect the environment of other states. In its Advisory Opinion on the *Legality of the Threat or Use of Nuclear Weapons*, the ICJ referred to its Order of 1995 in the *Nuclear Tests* case between France and New Zealand. In this instance, the ICJ made this order "without prejudice to the obligations of States regarding the respect and protection of the natural environment."[193] On this basis, in its 1996 Advisory Opinion, the ICJ found that a general duty of a state to respect and protect the environment applies during armed conflict. It affirms in this context that: "[w]hile the existing international law relating to the protection and safeguarding of the environment does not specifically prohibit the use of nuclear weapons, it indicates important environmental factors that are properly to be taken into account in

191 Principle 21 of the Stockholm Declaration (1972) and Principle 2 of the Rio Declaration on Environment and Development (1992).

192 ICJ, *Legality of the Threat or Use of Nuclear Weapons, Advisory Opinion, I.C.J. Reports 1996*, p. 226, at p. 242, para. 29.

193 ICJ, *Request for an Examination of the Situation in Accordance with Paragraph 63 of the Court's Judgment of 20 December 1974 in the* Nuclear Tests (New Zealand *v.* France) *Case, I.C.J. Reports 1995*, p. 228, at p. 306, para. 64.

the context of the implementation of the principles and rules of the law applicable in armed conflict."[194]

The general obligation of states to respect the environment in other states is broader than the duty not to cause harm to the environment in the territories beyond the territorial jurisdiction of a state. This obligation includes protection of the environment in any state, regardless of the 'control' exercised by states' authorities.[195]

The principle of equitable and reasonable use is a fundamental tenet of international water law.[196] According to the 1997 UN Watercourses Convention, states:

> shall in their respective territories utilize an international watercourse in an equitable and reasonable manner. In particular, an international watercourse shall be used and developed by watercourse States with a view to attaining optimal and sustainable utilization thereof and benefits therefrom, taking into account the interests of the watercourse States concerned, consistent with adequate protection of the watercourse.[197]

Some instruments related to armed conflicts make reference to the principle of equitable and reasonable utilization, like the Bahrain Environmental Code of Conduct for the Middle East of 1994 developed by the Multilateral Working Group on the Environment of the Middle East peace process, the Declaration of Principles between Israel and the Palestinian Authority of 1993[198] and the

194 ICJ, *Legality of the Threat or Use of Nuclear Weapons, Advisory Opinion, I.C.J. Reports 1996*, p. 226, at p. 242, para. 33.

195 Philippe Antoine, 'Droit international humanitaire et protection de l'environnement en temps de conflit armé', *International Review of the Red Cross*, Vol. 74 (798) (1992), pp. 537–558, at p. 539.

196 In the *Gabčíkovo-Nagymaros* case, the Court considered that: "Czechoslovakia, by unilaterally assuming control of a shared resource, and thereby depriving Hungary of its right to an equitable and reasonable share of the natural resources of the Danube—with the continuing effects of the diversion of these waters on the ecology of the riparian area of the Szigetkoz—failed to respect the proportionality which is required by international law." ICJ, *Gabčíkovo-Nagymaros Project (Hungary/Slovakia), Judgment, I.C.J Reports 1997*, p. 7, at para. 85.

197 Article 5 of the UN Watercourses Convention. See Lucius Caflisch, 'La Convention du 21 mai 1997 sur l'utilisation des cours d'eau à des fins autres que la navigation', *Annuaire français de droit international*, Vol. 43 (1997), pp. 751–798, at p. 751.

198 Article 1 of Annex III, Protocol on Israeli-Palestinian Cooperation in Economic and Development Programs to the Declaration of Principles on Interim Self-Government Arrangements (13 September 1993), http://www.incore.ulst.ac.uk/services/cds/agreements/pdf/is25.pdf, last accessed on 15 October 2016.

Peace Treaty between Israel and Jordan of 1994.[199] In particular, the Bahrain Environmental Code of Conduct for the Middle East of 1994 affirms that:

> Natural resources of the region should be utilized on a sustainable basis, and unique environmental resources to the region should be preserved. The parties will strive for a fair and just utilization and coordinated management policies of the shared natural resources in the region.[200]

Notwithstanding these agreements, problems are manifold. For example, despite the 1993 Declaration of Principles and the 1994 Bahrain Environmental Code of Conduct, the Interim Agreement between Israel and Palestine of 1995 did not recognize Palestine's rights to access the waters of the Jordan River.

III *The Practice of International Watercourse Treaties and Armed Conflicts*

This section will look at certain treaties on international watercourses which contain provisions on armed conflicts (Part 1). It will then deal with the normative influence of IHL on these treaties (Part 2). Finally, it will examine the practice of certain international regimes on transboundary water resources during armed conflict (Part 3), before turning to the case of the Danube River (Part 4).

1 The Specific Solutions Found in International Watercourse Treaties

Certain early twentieth century treaties governing the law of international watercourses contain provisions on the effects of armed conflicts. For instance, the 1921 Statute on the Regime of Navigable Waterways of International Concern and the 1923 Convention relating to the Development of Hydraulic Power affecting more than one State both assert that they will "continue in force" in times of war "so far as [... permitted]" by the rights and duties of belligerents.[201] In contrast to these early twentieth century agreements, international

---

199 Article 6 of the Israel-Jordan Peace Treaty and Annex II on Water and Related Matters (26 October 1994), http://www.mfa.gov.il/MFA/ForeignPolicy/Peace/Guide/Pages/Israel-Jordan%20Peace%20Treaty.aspx, last accessed on 20 January 2016.

200 Bahrain Environmental Code of Conduct for the Middle East (1994), http://www.mofa.go.jp/region/middle_e/peaceprocess/ewg/bcc.pdf, last accessed on 15 October 2016.

201 Article 9 of the 1923 Convention relating to the Development of Hydraulic Power affecting more than one State also provides: "This Convention does not prescribe the rights and duties of belligerents and neutrals in time of war. The Convention shall, however, continue in force in time of war so far as such rights and duties permit." League of Nations, *Treaty Series*, Vol. 36, p. 76. Article 15 of the Statute on the Regime of Navigable Waterways of International Concern of 1921 provides: "This Statute does not prescribe the rights and

watercourse instruments in the last few decades have provided for a specific approach to armed conflict. Their distinctive feature consists in their reference to the standards of IHL. Thus, Article 29 of the 1997 UN Watercourses Convention provides that:

> International watercourses and related installations, facilities and other works shall enjoy the protection accorded by the principles and rules of international law applicable in international and non-international armed conflict and shall not be used in violation of those principles and rules.[202]

As the Commentary explains, Article 29 of the 1997 UN Watercourses Convention

> does not lay down any new rule. It simply serves as a reminder that the principles and rules of international law applicable in international and internal armed conflict contain important provisions concerning international watercourses and related works.[203]

The application of IHL and international water law has the potential to promote the protection of water resources. Observing international watercourse treaties reduces the risk of serious damage to other riparian states. Other parties to the watercourse treaty must "ensure that activities within their jurisdiction and control respect the environment of other States."[204] Compliance with international watercourse treaty obligations plays a key role in the implementation of this general obligation.

2 The Normative Impact of International Humanitarian Law on International Water Law

Both the 1997 UN Watercourses Convention and the ILC's 2008 Draft Articles on the Law of Transboundary Aquifers contain a provision that explicitly refers to

duties of belligerents and neutrals in time of war. The Statute shall, however, continue in force in time of war so far as such rights and duties permit". League of Nations, *Treaty Series*, Vol. 7, p. 35.

202 Article 29 of the UN Watercourses Convention.

203 Draft Articles on the Law of the Non-Navigational Uses of International Watercourses, *Yearbook of the International Law Commission*, vol. II, Part 2 (1994), Article 29, p. 138.

204 ICJ, *Legality of the Threat or Use of Nuclear Weapons, Advisory Opinion, I.C.J. Reports 1996*, p. 226, at p. 242, para. 29.

humanitarian law and that has the same wording in both texts. The commentary to Article 29 of the UN Watercourses Convention, moreover, cites all the relevant provisions of humanitarian law,[205] even though, in some cases, only an indirect reference to IHL is included in the UN Watercourses Convention. Article 10 (2) provides that "[i]n the event of a conflict between uses of an international watercourse, it shall be resolved with reference to articles 5 to 7, with special regard being given to the requirements of *vital human needs.*"[206] As the commentary to the Convention indicates, this last expression is inspired by IHL, particularly the 'Martens clause'. According to the commentary,

> [i]n cases [of armed conflict] not covered by a specific rule [of humanitarian law protecting the environment], certain fundamental protections are afforded by the 'Martens clause'. [...] In essence, [this clause] provides that even in cases not covered by specific international agreements, civilians and combatants remain under the protection and authority of the principles of international law derived from established custom, from the principles of humanity and from the dictates of public conscience. The same general principle is expressed in article 10 of the draft articles, which provides that in reconciling a conflict between uses of an international watercourse, special attention is to be paid to the requirements of vital human needs.[207]

Although the normative influence of humanitarian law on the 1997 UN Watercourses Convention is indirect, it is not insignificant since the Convention references IHL as a key element in defining—or, in other words, interpreting—the expression 'vital human needs.'

The effect of armed conflicts can be seen in the substantive rules of the UN Watercourses Convention. When the ILC was developing the law on the uses of international watercourses, the Special Rapporteurs explicitly indicated their interest in taking into account the impact of armed conflicts on international watercourse regimes.[208] Special Rapporteur Stephen C. McCaffrey, in particular, suggested adopting a principle that international watercourses and related

205 Draft Articles on the Law of the Non-Navigational Uses of International Watercourses, supra, note 203, p. 131.

206 Italics added.

207 Draft Articles on the Law of the Non-Navigational Uses of International Watercourses, supra, note 203, p. 131.

208 See Third report by Special Rapporteur Stephen M. Schwebel, *Yearbook of the International Law Commission*, vol. II, Part 1 (1982), p. 65 and Sixth report by Special

installations were inviolable in times of armed conflict.[209] According to the Special Rapporteur, such a principle would strengthen IHL by guaranteeing a more extensive protection of water resources. The Commission, however, rejected this principle. It was too far-reaching for several of its members given that it would have prohibited using rivers for military ends, such as for transporting troops or military equipment.[210] Following criticisms of the Special Rapporteur's proposal, the 1994 Draft Articles and the 1997 Convention were ultimately limited to referencing the rules of humanitarian law.

That being said, some of the Convention's provisions seem to have been drafted in order to resolve potential issues that would arise primarily in the case of armed conflicts. For example, Article 30 provides that "[i]n cases where there are serious obstacles to direct contacts between watercourse States, the States concerned shall fulfil their obligations of cooperation provided for in the present Convention, including exchange of data and information, notification, communication, consultations and negotiations, through any indirect procedure accepted by them."[211] The Commentary expressly mentions armed conflicts and the absence of diplomatic relations as circumstances raising 'serious obstacles' to fulfilling the obligation of cooperation as defined by Article 30. The Article provides that in such cases the affected states may use other channels of communication. Third-party countries, armistice commissions or the good offices of international organizations are some examples of other channels of communication. Watercourse states may therefore exchange data and information via international organizations. In this sense, the Convention itself contemplates a specific regime applicable when it is impossible, due to an armed conflict, to perform some of the obligations it contains. This regime seems to be a form of treaty accommoda-

Rapporteur Stephen C. McCaffrey, *Yearbook of the International Law Commission*, vol. II, Part 1 (1990), p. 57.

209 In his sixth report, Special Rapporteur Stephen C. McCaffrey proposed a Draft Article that provided: "International watercourses and related installations, facilities and other works shall be used exclusively for peaceful purposes consonant with the principles enshrined in the Charter of the United Nations and shall be inviolable in time of international as well as internal armed conflicts." *Yearbook of the International Law Commission*, vol. II, Part 1 (1990), p. 57 (Article 28).

210 Summary records of the meetings of the forty-third session, 2229th meeting, 25 June 1991, *Yearbook of the International Law Commission*, vol. I (1991), p. 143.

211 The Commentary notes that the watercourse states may use the good offices of international organizations to meet their obligations of cooperation under the Convention. Draft Articles on the Law of the Non-Navigational Uses of International Watercourses, supra, note 203, pp. 131–132.

tion from Article 61 of the Vienna Convention on the Law of Treaties, which addresses impossibility of performance resulting from the outbreak of an armed conflict.

This kind of regime matters because it guarantees that watercourse information continues to be exchanged during armed conflicts. Furthermore, conducting post-conflict environmental assessments on potential damage to international watercourses fits into this framework. These assessments allow parties to an armed conflict that have not yet signed a peace agreement to exchange information on water resources. The post-conflict environmental assessments conducted by UNEP are worth mentioning in this context.[212]

3 The Application of International Watercourse Treaties in Times of Armed Conflict

In the Commentary to its 2011 Draft Articles on the Effects of Armed Conflicts on Treaties, the ILC did not mention the existing international practice of continuing to enforce international watercourse treaties in times of armed conflict. Nevertheless, the Mekong, Indus, and Senegal Rivers were the sites of interesting illustrations, discussed in Case Study 12, of the continued application of international watercourse treaties during armed conflicts.

> The regime regarding the Mekong River[213] emerged in an historical context marked by the Indochina war and the Vietnam conflict.[214] After the French armed forces withdrew in 1954, Laos, Thailand, Cambodia and Vietnam signed a Convention in 1957 to establish the 'Committee for Co-ordination of Investigations of the Lower Mekong Basin.'[215] The subsequent armed conflicts did not cause any interruptions in the Committee's meetings. In the 1960s, the Committee even completed studies on the different uses of the Mekong and facilitated the gathering of information on the river's topography and hydrology.[216] Between 1957 and 1975, the Committee

212 See UNEP, supra, note 65.

213 The Mekong rises in China and flows through Myanmar, Laos, Cambodia, Thailand and Vietnam.

214 Stephen C. McCaffrey, *The Law of International Watercourses* (Oxford University Press, 2007), p. 285.

215 The Convention that establishes the Committee for Co-ordination of Investigations of the Lower Mekong Basin is reproduced *in*, Luc Lacroze, *L'aménagement du Mékong (1957–1997). L'échec d'une grande ambition?* (L'Harmattan, 1998), pp. 216–219.

216 Vanessa Richard, *La coopération sur la gestion des cours d'eau internationaux en Asie* (La Documentation française, 2005), p. 75.

benefitted from substantial funding from various sources, notably the United Nations and states like France and the United States,[217] funding which allowed it to conduct studies on the construction of dams on the Mekong.[218] The armed conflict that lasted from 1964 to 1975 did not lead to the termination or suspension of the treaty establishing the Mekong River Committee; on the contrary, the Committee continued to meet and conduct studies on the Mekong's development.[219]

The Indus River constitutes another interesting example. When British India was divided into the dominions of India and Pakistan in 1947, the partition of Punjab[220] created a conflict between the two countries.[221] This region, rich in waters flowing from the Indus River, was divided between the two countries. After years of negotiations assisted by the mediation efforts of the World Bank, the two countries ultimately adopted the Indus Waters Treaty in 1960.[222] The two wars between India and Pakistan, from 1965 to 1966 and from 1971 to 1972, did not cause the suspension or the termination of the treaty.[223] Tensions between the two countries did not prevent the Permanent Indus Commission from meeting and taking decisions on water management.

A final example of relevance involves the Senegal River. The relationship between two of the four riparian countries, i.e. Mauritania and Senegal, has on occasion been strained by the fact that the river delineates their common border. The 1972 Convention Concerning the Status of the Senegal River and the Convention Establishing the Organization for the Development of the Senegal River (in French the *Organisation pour la mise en valeur du fleuve Sénégal*) established a joint governance regime between Mauritania, Senegal and Mali.

217 Ibid., p. 81.

218 Greg Browder & Leonard Ortolano, 'The Evolution of an International Water Resources Management Regime in the Mekong River Basin', *Natural Resources Journal*, Vol. 40 (2000), pp. 499–531, at p. 507.

219 Richard, supra, note 216, p. 82. The Committee did not meet in 1976 and 1977.

220 Punjab was divided into two: East Punjab, located in India, and West Punjab, located in Pakistan. Salman M.A. Salman & Kishor Uprety, *Conflict and Cooperation on South Asia's International Rivers. A Legal Perspective*, (Kluwer/The World Bank, 2003), p. 41.

221 McCaffrey, supra, note 209, p. 289.

222 Indus Waters Treaty, Karachi, 19 September 1960, United Nations, *Treaty Series*, Vol. 419, p. 126. See Salman M.A. Salman, 'The Mediation of International Water Disputes—The Indus, the Jordan and the Nile Basins Interventions', *in*, Laurence Boisson de Chazournes; Christina Leb & Mara Tignino (eds.), *International Law and Freshwater. The Multiple Challenges* (Edward Elgar, 2013), pp. 360–405, at pp. 369–378.

223 Undala Alam, 'India and Pakistan's Truculent Cooperation: Can it Continue?' *in*, ibid., pp. 406–420.

Despite disagreements and tensions between Senegal and Mauritania between the late 1980s and the early 1990s, the joint governance of the Senegal River was not affected.[224]

Case Study 12: The Mekong, Indus, and Senegal River Cases.

As these examples illustrate, it is not rare for watercourse states to apply international watercourse treaties despite periods of armed conflict. This can be explained by the nature of the conflicts and the political relations between the watercourse states. Natural conditions must also be taken into account in order to understand continuity in cooperation between watercourse states during armed conflicts. For example, the scarcity of water may encourage the parties to cooperate in this vital area while also creating riparian tensions. Similarly, the continued implementation of the 1960 Indus Waters Treaty between India and Pakistan in times of armed conflict represents an example of cooperation between two countries whose relationship has been very strained over several issues.[225] Because of the vital nature of water resources and their uses, watercourse countries appear to be willing to continue to cooperate even in times of armed conflict. The termination or suspension of international watercourse treaties would endanger the mutual rights and obligations of treaty parties.

4 The Danube River and Armed Conflicts

During an armed conflict, treaties on navigation may continue to be applied by the parties. An example is the international regime on navigation established regarding the Danube River. The Danube River basin has been ravaged by war.[226] The watercourse became the object of an international regime established

224 See Convention Concerning the Status of the Senegal River and the Convention Establishing the Organization for the Development of the Senegal River (11 March 1972), FAO, Legislative Study No. 61, 1997, http://www.fao.org/docrep/W7414B/w7414b08.htm, last accessed on 15 October 2016.

225 See James Kraska, 'Sustainable Development is Security: The Role of Transboundary River Agreements as a Confidence Building Measure (CBM) in South Asia', *Yale Journal of International Law*, Vol. 28 (2003), pp. 465–503.

226 See Mara Tignino, 'L'incidence des conflits armés sur le régime des fleuves internationaux', *in*, Bogdan Aurescu & Alain Pellet (eds.), *L'actualité du droit des fleuves internationaux* (Pedone, 2010), pp. 187–201.

by the 1856 Paris Treaty and the 1921 Paris Convention.[227] The International Commission on the Danube[228] continued to meet before and during the two World Wars.[229] During the Second World War, in particular, the Commission established that the regime is inviolable and that navigation on the Danube should remain free. In April 1940, a meeting of the states' representatives to the International Commission on the Danube concluded with a resolution to limit the exchange of materials that could be used for military purposes. The Resolution states:

> Given the fundamental principle of the status of the Danube on the freedom of navigation on the Danube and the need to ensure that no obstacle should limit the safety of the navigation [... and] [t]aking into account also the joint declarations and proposals by Delegates of the riparian States currently represented in the International Commission of the Danube [...], given the exceptional circumstances of today, only the vessels used for the navigation of transport of people and goods will be allowed to navigate in the Danube. The transit of arms, munitions and explosives will not be admitted to navigate in the Danube without the prior permission of the transit State.[230]

As it was adopted in 1940 by Germany, Italy, France, the United Kingdom and Romania, this resolution demonstrates that hostilities did not impede the meetings and functioning of the Commission. The Commission therefore played a role in limiting the impacts of the war on the Danube River.[231] As Sir Gerald Gray Fitzmaurice has noted, international agreements that ensure the freedom of navigation on international watercourses are not affected by a war.[232]

After the Second World War, a new treaty, the Convention regarding the Regime of Navigation on the Danube, was adopted in Belgrade on 18 August

---

227 Paris Treaty of 30 March 1856, *Consolidated Treaty Series* (Dobbs Ferry, NY: Oceana, 1967), Vol. 114, p. 409. Paris Convention of 23 July 1921, League of Nations, *Treaty Series*, Vol. 26, p. 173.

228 Article XV of the Paris Treaty of 1856 established the Commission.

229 Pascale Costa, 'Les effets de la guerre sur les traités relatifs au Danube, dans le cadre d'une étude globale du droit conventionnel du Danube', *in*, Ralph Zacklin & Lucius Caflisch (eds.), *The Legal Regime of International Rivers and Lakes* (Martinus Nijhoff, 1981), pp. 203–245, at p. 232.

230 European Commission of the Danube, Session of May 1940, Galatz, Protocol No. 1394, p. 363 (translation by the author).

231 Costa, supra, note 228, p. 232.

232 Gerald Gray Fitzmaurice, 'The Juridical Clauses of Peace Treaties', *Collected Courses of the Hague Academy of International Law*, Vol. 73 (1948-II), pp. 255–367, at pp. 316–317.

1948. The Convention established the Danube Commission.[233] The regime pertaining to the Danube River also includes an instrument whose purpose is to protect the watercourse environment. The 1994 Convention on Co-operation for the Protection and Sustainable Use of the River Danube ('1994 Danube Convention') establishes the international commission tasked with protecting the international watercourse.[234]

The Danube Commission played a key role during the conflict in the former Yugoslavia, as further elaborated in Case Study 13.

The United Nations Security Council, acting under Chapter VII, established a sanctions regime against the Federal Republic of Yugoslavia (Serbia and Montenegro). In Resolution 820 of 1993, the Security Council decided that "no vessels registered in the Federal Republic of Yugoslavia" or "in which a majority or controlling interest is held by a person or undertaking in or operating from the Federal Republic of Yugoslavia" would be permitted "to pass through installations, including river locks or canals within the territory of Member States."[235]

The Security Council's ban on Yugoslavian ships had an impact on the Iron Gates power and navigation system located between Serbia and Romania.[236] This installation, which includes locks, must be maintained by both states. Given the Security Council sanctions, Yugoslavian vessels could no longer contribute the work necessary to keep the installation in good repair. The poor maintenance of the Iron Gates locks compromised navigation on the length of the Danube River.

Between 1993 and 1995, the Danube Commission, aware of the risks created by the Security Council sanctions restricting free navigation on the Danube, stressed that it was important for Yugoslavian vessels to participate in the maintenance of the Iron Gates lock. Based on information provided by the Danube Commission, the Security Council decided in 1995 to make an exception to the

233 The Commission was set up by Article 5 of the 1948 Convention.

234 Article 18 of the Convention.

235 Resolution S/RES/820 (1993), para. 16. See also Resolution S/RES/787 (1992), para. 10.

236 This work includes electricity production and navigation systems. See the Agreement between the Socialist Federal Republic of Yugoslavia and the Romanian People's Republic relating to the establishment and operation of the Iron Gates Water Power and Navigation System on the River Danube (30 November 1963). United Nations, *Treaty Series*, Vol. 512, p. 3.

sanctions regime restricting freedom of navigation and allow Yugoslavian vessels to maintain the Iron Gates lock.[237] The Danube Commission was to monitor the work to ensure that the authorized exemptions fulfilled the Security Council's purpose.[238] Thus, in spite of the armed conflict gripping former Yugoslavia in the early 1990s, the navigation regime established by the 1948 Belgrade Convention remained in force.

Freedom of navigation on the Danube River is critically important to riparian countries and to some non-riparian countries, like Russia. The Security Council emphasized the importance of freedom of navigation on this international watercourse in a Resolution that stressed the need to "promote free and unhindered navigation on the Danube."[239] The Security Council's call to re-establish free navigation on the Danube underlines the importance of respecting this principle in times of armed conflict.

Case Study 13: The Danube Case during the Conflict in ex-Yugoslavia.

During the 1999 Kosovo conflict, the Danube Commission established by the 1948 Belgrade Convention also played a significant role in ensuring respect for the principle of freedom of navigation during the conflict, as described in Case Study 14.[240]

237 Declaring that this "will require an exemption from the provisions of paragraph 16 of resolution 820 (1993) and acting, in this respect, under Chapter VII of the Charter of the United Nations," the Security Council "decides that the use of the locks of the Iron Gates I system on the left hand bank of the Danube by vessels (a) registered in the Federal Republic of Yugoslavia (Serbia and Montenegro) or (b) in which a majority or controlling interest is held by a person or undertaking in or operating from the Federal Republic of Yugoslavia (Serbia and Montenegro) shall be permitted in accordance with this resolution." Resolution S/RES/992 (1995), para. 1.

238 The Council further decided that the exemption from sanctions would "come into force on the day following [its] receipt [...] of a report by the Danube Commission that they are satisfied that preparations for the repairs to the locks of the Iron Gates I system on the right hand bank of the Danube have been completed." Resolution S/RES/992 (1995), para. 2.

239 Resolution S/RES/992 (1995), Preamble.

240 Minutes of the meetings of the Danube Commission, Fiftieth meeting, 1992, Vol. 50, CD/SES/50/12, pp. 270–272.

The debris from destroyed bridges on the Danube and the risks linked to unexploded munitions in the river hindered navigation on the watercourse for several years. The interruption of navigation brought serious economic implications for river transport and freight companies in Danube riparian states.[241] The Danube Commission[242] and the European Commission financed a project to clear debris and unexploded munitions in order to re-establish navigation on the Danube.[243]

This was made possible thanks to an International Fund for the Clearance of the Fairway of the Danube administered by both institutions.[244] The assistance of these international institutions made it possible to rebuild the bridges destroyed in the war and re-establish navigation on the Danube in the Yugoslavian sections of the river.

Case Study 14: The Danube and the Kosovo Conflict.

The armed conflicts of the 1990s in the former Yugoslavia damaged not only navigation on the Danube, but also its environment. In 1999, the river's environment suffered due to NATO air force bombings on industrial installations on

241 See 'Indemnisation des entreprises allemandes de navigation fluviale et de fret sur le Danube, en raison de l'interruption du trafic sur la partie yougoslave du Danube', *Official Journal of the European Union*, No. 374 E (28 December 2000), p. 0068. *See* also 'Kosovo', supra, note 9, p. 37.

242 In 1999, the Danube Commission adopted a decision emphasizing the significant financial losses caused by restrictions on freedom of navigation and requested the help of international organizations and financial institutions to clear and re-establish navigation in the fairway of the Danube in the Yugoslavian portions of the river. The decision asserts: "Following the interruption of navigation on the Danube, the member States of the Danube Commission suffered great financial losses. [...] The Commission considers it necessary to actively contribute [...] to the re-establishment of free and safe navigation on the Danube. [...] The member countries must face the task of clearing and re-establishing the freeway of the Danube, which is impossible without the assistance of international organisations and financial institutions." Minutes of the Danube Commission, Fifty-seventh meeting, Vol. 57, CD/SES/57/65 (1999), p. 67 (translation by the author).

243 The 1948 Convention regarding the regime of navigation on the Danube provides for the establishment of the Danube Commission (Article 5) (18 August 1948), United Nations, *Treaty Series*, Vol. 33, p. 196.

244 See 'Persistance des entraves à la navigation sur le Danube causées par la guerre de 1999 en Serbie', *Official Journal of the European Union*, No. 192 E (14 August 2003), pp. 0040–0041. See also 'Proposition de décision du Conseil relative à la contribution communautaire au Fonds international pour le "Déblaiement du chenal du Danube"' (2001/C 120 E/01) COM (2000) 317 final. 2000/0125(CNS), *Official Journal of the European Union*, No. C 120 (24 April 2001), pp. 1–2.

the banks of the Danube and its tributaries. The United Nations Environment Programme's post-conflict environmental assessment report on the 1999 Kosovo conflict highlighted the regional impact of the damage to the international watercourse.[245] The Danube is protected not only by its own specific instruments but also by international environmental treaties. The 1971 Ramsar Convention, for instance, protects the Danube River delta. The 1992 Biodiversity Convention also protects the fauna and flora of this international watercourse. The Danube River's ecosystem is thus protected by MEAs that remain in force during an armed conflict.[246]

The Danube example reveals the complexity of this international river's legal regime, a regime which includes both specific navigation and environmental treaties as well as multilateral agreements. The Danube case also illustrates that such agreements continue to apply during an armed conflict.

IV *Conclusion*

The relationship between humanitarian law and international water law can be understood as a normative exchange between two bodies of law. The exchanges take the form of obligations in international water instruments that enshrine principles drawn from international humanitarian law, such as the Martens clause principle requiring attention to 'vital human needs' in case of a conflict between the various uses of an international watercourse. At the same time, the wartime protection of water resources and installations must be interpreted and applied in light of a vast body of norms that includes norms from both IHL and international water law.

Armed conflicts do not entail the suspension or the extinction *ipso facto* and *ipso jure* of water agreements. Unlike cultural property, water is not protected by a specific conventional instrument defining the rules for the protection of water during armed conflict. Nevertheless, the efforts of the ILA and ILC signal the beginning of a universal codification regarding the protection of water resources in times of armed conflict. In this regard, the reference in Article 29 of the UN Watercourses Convention to the "principles and rules of international law applicable in international and non-international armed conflict" exemplifies the interaction between international water law and IHL.

Notwithstanding this legal architecture, when viewed through the prism of international water law, it becomes evident that protection of the environment of water resources during armed conflicts must be strengthened. In this

245 'Kosovo', supra, note 9, p. 4.

246 See Article 7 and Appendix, issue (g) of the ILC's Draft Articles on the Effects of Armed Conflicts on Treaties, supra, note 153.

context, institutional mechanisms on the management of the uses of transboundary water resources may play a significant role. The case of the Danube Commission offers an interesting example in this regard. The interplay between IHL, international environmental law and international water law calls for a coherent and comprehensive protection of water resources. As discussed in the following section, human rights law illuminates another facet of the relationship between water and armed conflicts, bringing into focus the protection of the rights of individuals and communities to access to fresh water.

C The Protection of Water under Human Rights Law

Water increasingly occupies an important place in the framework of human rights law. In 2010, the UN General Assembly and the Human Rights Council adopted two resolutions signalling the recognition of the right to water in international law.[247] These two United Nations resolutions recognize not only the human right to water but also the human right to sanitation.[248] In 2015, the UN General Assembly recognized the human right to sanitation as a distinct human right.[249]

After having analysed the protection of access to water in instruments of human rights law and international water law as well as the application of the right to water during armed conflicts (Part I), the monograph will look at the relationship between this right and the protection of the environment (Part II) and the contribution of the United Nations investigatory mechanisms to the definition of the human right to water (Part III).

I *Access to Water in Human Rights Law*

In 2002, the UN Committee on Economic, Social and Cultural Rights adopted General Comment No. 15 on the Right to Water, which states that the right to water is implicitly recognized in Article 11.1 on the right to an adequate standard of living and Article 12.1 on the right to health of the 1966 International

247 General Assembly, The human right to water and sanitation, A/RES/64/292 (28 July 2010); Human Rights Council, Human rights and access to safe drinking water and sanitation, A/HRC/RES/15/9 (30 September 2010).

248 See also Committee on Economic, Social and Cultural Rights, Statement on the Right to Sanitation, E/C.12/2010/1 (November 2010).

249 General Assembly, The human rights to safe drinking water and sanitation, A/C.3/70/L.55/Rev.1 (2015).

Covenant on Economic, Social, and Cultural Rights ('ICESCR').[250] General Comment No. 15 is thus a key document providing an authoritative interpretation of Articles 11 and 12 of the ICESCR. States parties are guided by the General Comments prepared by the ESCR Committee.[251] The General Comments aim to clarify the content of the norms contained in the Covenant, aiding states in the preparation of their reports regarding the implementation of the rights protected by the Covenant, and informing activities of states and international actors that are likely to impact on economic, social and cultural rights.[252]

The following paragraphs will examine the normative content of the human right to water and the contours of its obligations (Part 1) and will study the inclusion of the human right to water in international water law (Part 2) as well as the relationship between this right and armed conflicts (Part 3).

1 Normative Content of the Human Right to Water

In General Comment No. 15, the ESCR Committee defined the right to water as entitling "everyone to sufficient, safe, acceptable, physically accessible and affordable water for personal and domestic uses."[253] The human right to water entails three types of obligations: obligations to 'respect', 'protect' and 'fulfil.' The obligation to 'respect' requires states to not take any measures that would prevent individuals from enjoying their right to safe drinking water.[254] The obligation to 'protect' requires measures by the state to ensure that third

250 Committee on Economic, Social and Cultural Rights (ESCR Committee), General Comment No. 15 on the Right to Water, UN Doc. E/C.12/2002/11 (26 November 2002).

251 On the role of the UN Committee on Economic, Social and Cultural Rights as a quasi-judicial body, see M. Tignino, 'Quasi-Judicial Bodies', *in*, Catherine Brölmann & Yannick Radi (eds.), *Research Handbook on the Theory and Practice of International Law-Making* (Edward Elgar, 2016), pp. 242–260.

252 According to the ESCR Committee: "Through its general comments, the Committee endeavours to make the experience gained through the examination of States' reports available for the benefit of all States parties in order to assist and promote their further implementation of the Covenant; to draw the attention of the States parties to insufficiencies disclosed by a large number of reports; to suggest improvements in the reporting procedures; and to stimulate the activities of the States parties, international organizations and the specialized agencies concerned in achieving progressively and effectively the full realization of the rights recognized in the Covenant. Whenever necessary, the Committee may, in the light of the experience of States parties and of the conclusions drawn there from, revise and update its general comments." Committee on Economic, Social and Cultural Rights, Working Methods, Report on the Forty-Fourth and Forty-Fifth Sessions (E/2011/22—E/C.12/2010/3) (21 May 2010), para. 57.

253 General Comment No. 15, supra, note 250, para. 2.

254 Ibid., para. 21.

parties do not interfere with the enjoyment of the right to water.[255] This obligation includes, for example, adopting the necessary and effective legislative and other measures to restrain third parties from denying equal access to adequate water and from polluting water resources. The obligation to 'fulfil' requires states to adopt the necessary measures directed towards the full realization of the right to water.[256] For example, this obligation includes according sufficient recognition of this right within national political and legal systems; adopting a national water strategy and plan of action to realize this right; ensuring that water is affordable for everyone; and facilitating improved and sustainable access to water, particularly in rural and deprived urban areas.

In July 2010, the United Nations General Assembly declared access to water as a fundamental human right and affirmed the relationship between the right to water and the right to sanitation. The General Assembly recognized "the right to safe and clean drinking water and sanitation as a human right that is essential for the full enjoyment of life and all human rights."[257] It further called on "States and international organizations to provide financial resources, build capacity and transfer technology, particularly in developing countries, in scaling up efforts to provide safe, clean, accessible and affordable drinking water and sanitation for all."[258] Two months later, the Human Rights Council, in keeping with the General Assembly resolution, underlined that the right to water and sanitation is derived not only from the right to an adequate standard of living but is also inextricably related to the right to health and the right to life and human dignity.[259] The two resolutions are an authoritative confirmation of an international consensus on the existence of a human right to water and sanitation in human rights law.

2 Instruments of International Water Law and the Human Right to Water

The right to water makes a limited appearance in the instruments on transboundary water resources.[260] The 2002 Charter of the Water of the Senegal River is the first international river basin convention explicitly recognizing the

255 Ibid., para. 23.

256 Ibid., para. 26.

257 UN General Assembly Resolution A/64/292 (28 July 2010).

258 Ibid.

259 Human Rights Council, A/HRC/RES/15/9 (30 September 2010).

260 On this topic, see Christina Leb, 'The Right to Water in a Transboundary Context: Seminal Trends', *Water International*, Vol. 37(2) (2012), pp. 640–653.

human right to water.[261] One of the Charter's objectives is to promote sustainable development and human rights in the development of the river basin. With regard to the Niger River, the riparian states have also adopted an agreement recognizing the right to water. The 2008 Water Charter of the Niger Basin lists the "right to water of basin populations" alongside other criteria defining a reasonable and equitable utilization.[262]

The UNECE Protocol on Water and Health to the 1992 Convention on the Protection and Use of Transboundary Watercourses and International Lakes contains several obligations related to access to drinking water and sanitation.[263] The Protocol includes aspects of the right to water such as availability, quality and accessibility. It also stipulates special protection for vulnerable groups in its affirmation that "equitable access to water, adequate in terms both of quantity and of quality, should be provided for all members of the population, especially those who suffer a disadvantage or social exclusion."[264] Despite the fact that the Protocol on Water and Health does not explicitly recognize the human right to safe drinking water, it demonstrates the implications of the human right to water on the management of international watercourses.

The 1997 UN Watercourses Convention and the 2008 ILC Draft Articles on Transboundary Aquifers follow an approach that ties securing of water resources to the realization of the right to water. In determining whether a specific use is "equitable and reasonable", states should take into account "the social and economic needs of the watercourse States concerned" and the "population dependent on the watercourse in each watercourse State."[265] In the case of a conflict between the various uses of water resources, the UN Watercourses Convention and the 2008 ILC Draft Articles point out that "special regard" must be "given to the requirements of vital human needs."[266]A Statement of

261 Article 4 of the Senegal Waters Charter (2002).

262 Article 4 of the Niger Basin Waters Charter (2008).

263 See Attila Tanzi, 'Reducing the Gap between International Water Law and Human Rights Law: The UNECE Protocol on Water and Health', *Review of European, Comparative & International Environmental Law* (*RECIEL*), Vol. 12(3) (2010), pp. 267–285.

264 Article 5 (k).

265 Article 6 (b) and (c).

266 Article 10 (2) of the 1997 UN Watercourses Convention stipulates that: "In the event of a conflict between uses of an international watercourse, it shall be resolved with reference to Articles 5 to 7, with special regard being given to the requirements of vital human needs." Article 5 (2) of the 2008 ILC Draft Articles reads as follows: "The weight to be given to each factor is to be determined by its importance with regard to a specific transboundary aquifer or aquifer system in comparison with that of other relevant factors. In determining what is equitable and reasonable utilization, all relevant factors are to be

Understanding issued by the Working Group clarified that in determining 'vital human needs', "special attention is to be paid to providing sufficient water to sustain human life, including both drinking water and water required for production of food in order to prevent starvation."[267] The human right to water entails obligations broader than the concept of 'vital human needs'. It includes the right of access to water and sanitation facilities on a non-discriminatory basis and the state's duty to take measures which prevent third parties from interfering in the enjoyment of the right to water.[268] The *Sudan Human Rights Organisation & Centre on Housing Rights and Evictions (COHRE) v. Sudan* case illustrates this point. In this decision of 2009, the African Commission on Human and Peoples' Rights referred to General Comment No. 14 of the Right to Health of the Committee on Economic, Social and Cultural Rights, stating that "States should also refrain from unlawfully polluting air, water and soil [...] during armed conflicts in violation of international humanitarian law [...] States should also ensure that third parties do not limit people's access to health-related information and services and the failure to enact or enforce laws to prevent the pollution of water [...] violates the right to health."[269]

The human right to water has a broader scope of the concept of 'vital human needs' included in universal instruments such as the UN Watercourses Convention and the ILC Draft Articles on the Law of Transboundary Aquifers, enshrining the principle of non-discrimination and the obligations 'to respect', 'to protect' and 'to fulfil.'

3 The Protection of the Human Right to Water in Times of Armed Conflict

In General Comment No. 15, the right to drinking water during armed conflicts is included among the 'obligations to respect' that states must follow. This assertion that "the right to water embraces those obligations by which States parties are bound under international humanitarian law" signifies the

---

considered together and a conclusion reached on the basis of all the factors. However, in weighing different kinds of utilization of a transboundary aquifer or aquifer system, special regard shall be given to vital human needs."

267 Report of the Sixth Committee convening as the Working Group of the Whole, A/51/869 (11 April 1997), para. 8.

268 Alistair Rieu-Clarke; Ruby Moynihan & Bjørn-Oliver Magsig, *UN Watercourses Convention. User's Guide*, (Center for Water Law, Policy and Science, University of Dundee, 2012), p. 131.

269 African Commission on Human and Peoples' Rights, *Sudan Human Rights Organisation & Centre on Housing Rights and Evictions (COHRE) v. Sudan*, Communication 279/03-296/05 (27 May 2009), para. 210, http://caselaw.ihrda.org/doc/279.03-296.05/, last accessed on 19 February 2016.

recognition of the close relationship between obligations embodied in human rights law and IHL.[270]

Limiting access to water supplies indispensable to the survival of the civilian population is a violation of both IHL and human rights law. In spite of views held by some states that human rights instruments do not apply during times of armed conflict, the jurisprudence of international courts, like the ICJ,[271] as well as UN bodies, have reiterated that they remain binding during situations of armed conflict.[272] Both the ESCR Committee and the Committee on the Rights of the Child addressed the issue of access to drinking water in occupied territory.[273]

In support of the argument that the obligations resulting from the ESCR Covenant are applicable in times of armed conflict, one may note that the ESCR Covenant contains no provisions for derogation in case of armed conflict. The only derogations from the Covenant that a state may invoke are stated in Article 4, which indicates that the limitations to the 1966 ESCR Covenant have to be "determined by law only in so far as this may be compatible with the nature of these rights and solely for the purpose of promoting the general welfare in a democratic society."[274] This establishes restrictive criteria for any derogation from the ESCR Covenant.[275]

The relevance of human rights instruments to questions of water protection during armed conflicts is limited by the fact that human rights instruments are generally considered to apply only within the jurisdiction of a signatory. This jurisdictional limitation has not, however, meant that these instruments are

270 General Comment No. 15, supra, note 250, paras. 21–22.

271 ICJ, *Legality of the Threat or Use of Nuclear Weapons, Advisory Opinion, I.C.J. Reports 1996*, p. 226, at para. 25; *Legal Consequences of the Construction of a Wall in the Occupied Palestinian Territory, Advisory Opinion, I.C.J. Reports 2004*, p. 136, at p. 178, para. 105; *Armed Activities on the Territory of the Congo (Democratic Republic of the Congo* v. *Uganda), Judgment, I.C.J. Reports 2005*, p. 168, at para. 216.

272 Sassòli, supra, note 156, p. 385; Droege, supra, note 156, p. 320.

273 ESCR Committee, Concluding Observations: Israel, E/C.12/1/Add.69 (31 August 2001), paras. 12–13; ESCR Committee, Concluding Observations: Israel, E/C.12/1/Add.90 (26 June 2003), para. 40; Committee on the Rights of the Child, Concluding Observations: Israel, CRC/C/15/Add.195 (9 October 2002), para. 51.

274 Article 4 of the ESCR Covenant.

275 In its Advisory Opinion on the *Legal Consequences of the Construction of a Wall in the Occupied Palestinian Territory*, the ICJ considered that restrictions to the 1966 Covenant may be invoked by states solely for the purpose of promoting the general welfare in a democratic society. *Legal Consequences of the Construction of a Wall in the Occupied Palestinian Territory, Advisory Opinion, I.C.J. Reports 2004*, p. 136, at para. 136.

not applied beyond national territory. Many international human rights instruments have clauses explicitly setting out their scope of application.[276] Other instruments, however,—including the International Covenant on Economic, Social and Cultural Rights—contain no such provisions.[277]

The extraterritorial application of human rights instruments has been analysed by the International Court of Justice in two cases: in the *Legal Consequences of the Construction of a Wall in the Occupied Palestinian Territory* advisory opinion[278] and the *Case Concerning Armed Activities on the Territory of the Congo*.[279] In both cases, the Court adopted a permissive approach to the extraterritorial application of human rights instruments. Although the ICESCR makes no reference to territory or jurisdiction, the ICJ interpreted the Covenant as applying extraterritorially to occupied territory.

Guaranteeing the human right to water against violations by a state in territory under its control may play an important role in mitigating the effects of

276 The International Covenant on Civil and Political Rights 1966 (ICCPR), as an example, provides that: "[e]ach State Party to the present Covenant undertakes to respect and to ensure to all individuals within its territory and subject to its jurisdiction the rights recognized in the present Covenant [...]". Article 2.1 of the Covenant on Civil and Political Rights. In addition, Article 2.1 of the Convention on the Rights of the Child provides that states parties "shall respect and ensure the rights set forth in the present Convention to each child within their jurisdiction [...]".

277 For further elaboration on this subject, see Fons Coomans, 'Some Remarks on the Extraterritorial Application of the International Covenant on Economic, Social and Cultural Rights', *in*, Fons Coomans & Menno T. Kamminga (eds.), *Extraterritorial Application of Human Rights Treaties* (Intersentia, 2004), pp. 183–199; Rolf Künnemann, 'Extraterritorial Application of the International Covenant on Economic, Social and Cultural Rights', ibid., pp. 201–231.

278 ICJ, *Legal Consequences of the Construction of a Wall in the Occupied Palestinian Territory, Advisory Opinion, I.C.J. Reports 2004*, p. 136, at pp. 179–181, paras. 109–113. In its Advisory Opinion, the Court stated that: "while the jurisdiction of States is primarily territorial, it may sometimes be exercised outside the national territory. Considering the object and purpose of the International Covenant on Civil and Political Rights, it would seem natural that, even when such is the case, State parties to the Covenant should be bound to comply with its provisions." (para. 109).

279 ICJ, *Armed Activities on the Territory of the Congo (Democratic Republic of the Congo* v. *Uganda), Judgment, I.C.J. Reports 2005*, p. 168, at para. 216. The Court concluded that both branches of international law, namely international human rights law and international humanitarian law, have to be taken into consideration. The Court further concluded that international human rights instruments are applicable "'in respect of acts done by a State in the exercise of its jurisdiction outside its own territory', particularly in occupied territories."

armed conflict on access to water. For example, one can consider the influence that an occupying power could exercise over the management, distribution, and extraction of water resources in a territory under its control. On several occasions, both the ESCR Committee and the Committee on the Rights of the Child have reminded the government of Israel of its obligations regarding access to an equitable distribution of water resources in the Occupied Palestinian Territories.[280]

Regional human rights bodies have taken a similar line on extraterritorial application. A case in point is the recognition of the extraterritorial application of the European Convention on Human Rights.[281] In the *Loizidou v. Turkey, Cyprus v. Turkey* and *Ilascu v. Moldova and Russia* cases, the European Court of Human Rights ('ECtHR') analysed Article 1 of the European Convention on Human Rights, stating that the concept of jurisdiction "is not restricted to national territory of the High Contracting Parties", but includes the territories on which a Party "exercises effective control."[282]

The most important criterion for evaluating the extraterritorial application of the European Convention on Human Rights is whether the state party is exercising effective control over a foreign territory. In a case concerning military operations by the armed forces of a state party to the Convention, the Court would be required to assess whether that criterion was met. In its 2005 *Issa* decision, the European Court considered that the concept of 'jurisdiction' under the Convention (obligation to respect human rights) was not restricted to the national territory of the contracting parties. Accountability in such situations stems from the fact that Article 1 of the Convention could not be interpreted to permit a contracting state to perpetrate violations of the Convention

280 ESCR Committee, Concluding Observations: Israel, E/C.12/1/Add.69 (31 August 2001), paras. 12–13; ESCR Committee, Concluding Observations: Israel, E/C.12/1/Add.90 (26 June 2003), para. 40; Committee on the Rights of the Child, Concluding Observations: Israel, CRC/C/15/Add.195 (9 October 2002), para. 51.

281 ECtHR, *Loizidou v. Turkey, Reports of Judgments and Decisions*, Series A 310, (Preliminary Objections), Judgment of 23 March 1995, paras. 62–64; *Loizidou v. Turkey, Reports of Judgments and Decisions 1996-VI*, (Merits), Judgment of 18 December 1996, paras. 52–56; *Cyprus v. Turkey, Reports of Judgments and Decisions 2001-IV*, Judgment of 10 May 2001, paras. 75–81; *Ilaşcu and others v. Moldova and Russia, Reports of Judgments and Decisions 2001-VII*, Judgment of 4 July 2004, para. 394. See also *Al-Skeini v. United Kingdom*, Judgment of 7 July 2011, para. 136.

282 See, for example, ECtHR, *Loizidou v. Turkey, Reports of Judgments and Decisions 1996–VI*, (Merits), Judgment of 18 December 1996, para. 52.

on the territory of another state, violations which it cannot commit on its own territory.[283]

Like the European Court of Human Rights, the Inter-American human rights mechanisms have considered the question of extraterritorial application. A state party to the 1969 American Convention on Human Rights must guarantee the Convention's rights and freedoms to any person within its jurisdiction.[284] In principle, a state exercises jurisdiction over its territory, thus circumscribing the limits of the Convention's application. The Inter-American bodies would certainly find justification for sanctioning violations by an agent of a state party, even if the individual concerned operated outside that state's territory. The decision of the Inter-American Commission in the case *Alejandre and Others v. Cuba* provides an example. In its reasoning, the Commission followed an approach similar to that of the European Court. The Commission pointed out:

> Because individual rights are inherent to the human being, all the American states are obligated to respect the protected rights of any person subject to their jurisdiction. Although this usually refers to persons who are within the territory of a state, in certain instances it can refer to extraterritorial actions, when the person is present in the territory of a state but subject to the control of another state, generally through the

283 In the *Issa* decision, the Court stated that: "the concept of 'jurisdiction' within the meaning of Article 1 of the Convention is not necessarily restricted to the national territory of the High Contracting Parties [...]. In exceptional circumstances, the acts of Contracting States performed outside their territory or which produce effects there ('extra-territorial act') may amount to exercise by them of their jurisdiction within the meaning of Article 1 of the Convention." The Court added that: "According to the relevant principles of international law, a State's responsibility may be engaged where, as a consequence of military action—whether lawful or unlawful—that State in practice exercises effective control of an area situated outside its national territory. The obligation to secure [...] the rights and freedoms set out in the Convention derives from the fact of such control, whether it be exercised directly, through its armed forces, or through a subordinate local administration." ECtHR, *Issa and Others v. Turkey*, Judgment of 30 March 2005, paras. 68–69, http://cmiskp.echr.coe.int/tkp197/view.asp?action=html&documentID=707749&portal=hbkm&source=externalbydocnumber%table=F69A27FD8FB86142BF01C1166DEA398649, last accessed on 20 January 2016.

284 According to Article 1 of the 1969 American Convention: "The States Parties to this Convention undertake to respect the rights and freedoms recognized herein and to ensure to all persons subject to their jurisdiction the free and full exercise of those rights and freedoms, without any discrimination for reasons of race, color, sex, language, religion, political or other opinion, national or social origin, economic status, birth, or any other social condition."

> actions of that state's agents abroad. In principle, the investigation refers not to the nationality of the alleged victim or his presence in a particular geographic area, but to whether, in those specific circumstances, the state observed the rights of a person subject to its authority and control.[285]

Although the cases reviewed do not concern the protection of water resources, they indicate how the main human rights instruments would be interpreted and their relationship with the issue of extraterritorial application.

II *The Human Right to Water and Protection of the Environment*

Although human survival is dependent on safeguarding the environment in which humans live, the body of legal texts elaborating the role of environmental protection in international human rights law remains modest.[286] There are, however, regional instruments for the protection of human rights that expressly codify the human right to a healthy environment, like the African Charter on Human and Peoples' Rights[287] and the Additional Protocol to the American Convention on Economic, Social and Cultural Rights.[288]

Recent years have brought a growing interest in the relationship between human rights law and protection of the environment. In 2012, the UN Human Rights Council appointed John Knox as Independent Expert on the issue of "human rights obligations relating to the enjoyment of a safe, clean, healthy and sustainable environment."[289] In his 2013 report, John Knox affirmed the

285 *Armando Alejandre Jr., Carlos Costa, Mario de la Pena y Pablo Morales v. Republic of Cuba*, Report No. 86/99, OEA/Ser.L/V/II.106 doc. 3 rev. 1999, para. 23 (footnotes omitted).

286 Mara Tignino, 'The Legal Regime of Natural Resources in Times of Armed Conflict and its Weaknesses', *in*, Yann Kebrat & Sandrine Maljean-Dubois (eds.), *The Transformation of International Environmental Law* (Hart & Pedone, 2011), pp. 193–207.

287 Article 24 states that "All peoples shall have the right to a general satisfactory environment favorable to their development." African (Banjul) Charter on Human and Peoples' Rights (27 June 1981), OAU Doc. CAB/LEG/67/3 rev.5, http://www.achpr.org/files/instruments/achpr/banjul_charter.pdf, last accessed on 15 October 2016.

288 Article 11 reads as follows: "1. Everyone shall have the right to live in a healthy environment and to have access to basic public services. 2. The State Parties shall promote the protection, preservation, and improvement of the environment. Article 12 (1) reads: Everyone has the right to adequate nutrition which guarantees the possibility of enjoying the highest level of physical, emotional and intellectual development." Additional Protocol to the American Convention on Human Rights in the Area of Economic, Social and Cultural Rights (17 November 1988), http://www.oas.org/juridico/english/treaties/a-52.html, last accessed on 15 October 2016.

289 Human Rights Council, A/HRC/RES/19/10 (22 March 2012). In 2015, John Knox was appointed as Special Rapporteur. Human Rights Council, A/HRC/RES/28/11 (7 April 2015).

principle that "environmental degradation can and does adversely affect the enjoyment of a broad range of human rights, including rights to life, health, food and water."[290] This reiterated the Human Rights Council's existing pronouncements that "environmental damage can have negative implications, both direct and indirect, for the effective enjoyment of human rights."[291] While not surprising, these affirmations underline the relationship between contamination and environmental pollution and the life and health of the population.

Recognizing the human right to water contributes to the protection of this natural resource. In particular, the Committee on Economic, Social and Cultural Rights, in its General Comment No. 15 on the right to water, construed the human right to water as encompassing the obligation to take steps "on a non-discriminatory basis to prevent threats to health from unsafe and toxic water conditions [...] States parties should ensure that natural water resources are protected from contamination by harmful substances and pathogenic microbes."[292]

At a regional level, decisions of the African Commission on Human and Peoples' Rights and the Inter-American Court of Human Rights elucidate the contours of the right to water and its relationship with other human rights, including the right to life.[293]

A notable case is the decision on the *Comunidad indígena Yakye Axa v. Paraguay* of 2005. The Inter-American Court of Human Rights bases its recognition of the right to water on General Comment No. 15. The Court interpreted the right to water as part of the right to property protected by the 1969 American Convention on Human Rights.[294] The Court noted that the

---

290 Human Rights Council, *Report of the Independent Expert on the Issue of Human Rights Obligations Relating to the Enjoyment of a Safe, Clean and Sustainable Environment*, A/HRC/22/43 (24 December 2012), para. 34.

291 Human Rights Council, A/HRC/RES/28/11 (26 March 2015).

292 General Comment No. 15, supra, note 250, para. 8.

293 African Commission on Human and Peoples' Rights, *Social and Economic Rights Actions Center and the Center for Economic and Social Rights v. Nigeria*, Communication 155/96 (27 October 2001), IACtHR, *Comunidad indígena Yakye Axa v. Paraguay* (17 June 2005), Series C No. 125, para. 167, IACtHR, *Case of the Sawhoyamaxa Indigenous Community v. Paraguay* (29 March 2006), Series C No. 125, para. 153.

294 See on the relationship between the protection of indigenous peoples' rights and the protection of property, Mara Tignino, 'Principle 23: The Environment of Oppressed People' *in*, Jorge E. Viñuales (ed.), *The Rio Declaration on Environment and Development* (Oxford University Press, 2015), pp. 557–568.

> Committee on Economic, Social and Cultural Rights has highlighted the special vulnerability of many groups of indigenous peoples whose access to ancestral lands has been threatened and, therefore, their possibility of access to means of obtaining food and clean water.[295]

Moreover, in this same case, the Inter-American Court underlines the relationship between the right to life and the right to water. Taking into account General Comment No. 15, expressly cited in the judgment,[296] the Court considers that the right to life guaranteed under Article 4 of the American Convention has been violated because the indigenous community has been deprived "of the possibility of access to their traditional means of subsistence, as well as to use and enjoyment of the natural resources necessary to obtain clean water."[297] This interpretation by the Court expanded the scope of the right to life to include the violation of the right to have access to essential natural resources, such as fresh water.

The African Commission on Human and Peoples' Rights has relied on the jurisprudence of the Inter-American Court. In particular, the Commission has interpreted both the Article 14 protection of property and the Article 21 right to dispose of wealth and resources of the African Charter so as to provide strong protection for indigenous peoples' rights to resources on their ancestral lands—even when the resources in question are not connected to survival or traditional practices.[298]

Turning to the European context, the case law of the European Court of Human Rights has addressed issues relating to the environment in connection with both the right to life[299] and the right to protection of private and family

---

295 IACtHR, *Comunidad indígena Yakye Axa v. Paraguay* (17 June 2005), Series C No. 125, para. 167.

296 Ibid., p. 90.

297 Ibid., para. 168.

298 African Commission on Human and Peoples' Rights, *Centre for Minority Rights Development (Kenya) and Minority Rights Group International on Behalf of Endorois Welfare Council v. Kenya* (4 February 2010), para. 267. Tignino (2015), supra, note 294, p. 565.

299 ECtHR, *Öneryildiz v. Turkey*, Collection (GC) No. 48939, ECHR, 2004-XII (30 November 2004), para. 90. In this judgment the Court recalled that the Convention's guarantee of the right to life imposes not only a negative obligation on State authorities to refrain from the arbitrary use of force, but also includes a positive obligation on States to take appropriate steps to safeguard the lives of those within their jurisdiction. This obligation extends to any activity, whether public or not, "in which the right to life may be at stake, and a fortiori in the case of industrial activities which by their very nature are dangerous, such as

life.[300] In particular, in the decision of *Tătar v. Romania* in 2009, the European Court concluded that Article 8 of the ECHR, dealing with the protection of private and family life, covered the health impacts caused by pollution generated by the Sasara gold mining operation.[301]

As these examples suggest, the protection of the environment and other human rights, like the right to life and the right to the protection of private and family life, can enhance access to water and sanitation and strengthen the role of the human right to water during armed conflicts and in occupied territories. These rights strongly circumscribe the scope of permissible limitations on access to water. Respect of the right to water requires that, during armed conflicts, the civilian population must have access to a sufficient quantity of drinking water. Protecting the right to water against the acts of a state in territory under its control may play an important role in limiting the impact on access to water caused by an armed conflict. For example, one could consider the control that an occupying power might exercise over the management, distribution, and extraction of water resources in a territory under its control. On several occasions, both the ESCR Committee and the Committee on the Rights of the Child have reminded the government of Israel of its obligations regarding access to an equitable distribution and management of water resources in the Occupied Palestinian Territories.[302]

---

the operation of waste-collection sites." (para. 71). See Dinah Shelton, 'Human Rights and the Environment: Substantive Rights', *in*, Malgosia Fitzmaurice; David M. Ong & Panos Merkouris (eds.), *Research Handbook on International Environmental Law* (Edward Elgar, 2011), pp. 265–283.

300 In the case of *López Ostra v. Spain*, the applicant complained of smoke emissions and noise caused by a sewage treatment plant near his home, which made living conditions unbearable for his family. The Court found that "severe environmental pollution may affect individuals' well-being and prevent them from enjoying their homes in such a way as to affect their private and family life adversely, without, however, seriously endangering their health." ECtHR, *López Ostra v. Spain, Reports Series A303-C,* Judgment of 9 December 1994, para. 51. See also *Guerra and others v. Italy, Reports 1998-I,* Judgment of 19 February 1998, para. 60.

301 In this case, the Court, "taking into account the findings of official reports [...], concludes that pollution generated by the activity of the Sasar mining operation could cause a deterioration in the quality of life for residents and, in particular, affect the well-being of the applicants and deny them the enjoyment of their homes in a manner detrimental to their private and family life." (translation by the author). Article 8 was therefore found to be applicable. ECtHR, *Case of Tătar v. Romania,* Judgment of 27 January 2009, para. 97.

302 ESCR Committee, Concluding Observations: Israel, E/C.12/1/Add.69 (31 August 2001), paras. 12–13; ESCR Committee, Concluding Observations; Israel, E/C.12/1/Add.90 (26 June

In occupied territories, the human right to water not only entitles the population to sufficient and safe water supplies, it also requires that an occupying power refrain from any practice that denies or limits equal access to adequate water. Non-discrimination and equality are key features of the human right to water and must be respected during armed conflicts and in occupied territories.

III *United Nations Investigatory Mechanisms and the Human Right to Water*

A further source of human rights norms affecting water comes from *ad hoc* investigative mechanisms. Such mechanisms established under a human rights mandate contribute to the development of the rules applicable to natural resources in armed conflicts. As an example, the 2006 Commission of Inquiry on Lebanon and the 2009 Fact-Finding Mission on the conflict in Gaza—each established by resolutions of the Human Rights Council—included in their final reports an assessment of the environmental damage caused by these conflicts.[303]

The Commission of Inquiry on Lebanon underscored the injury caused in both the short and long term to biological resources on the Lebanese coast as a result of oil spilled following the bombing of the Jiyeh facility.[304] The Fact-Finding Mission on the conflict in Gaza highlighted the risk of harm to the health of the population caused by the presence of unexploded cluster ordnances and other contaminants in the territory.[305] The presence of unexploded munitions and debris of war made it difficult for people to pursue their livelihoods and contaminated soil and water resources. The UN Fact-Finding Mission concluded that "the series of acts that deprive Palestinians in the Gaza Strip of their means of sustenance [...] and water could lead a competent court to find that the crime of persecution, a crime against humanity, has been committed."[306]

Inquiry commissions can find that an international crime has occurred, without identifying individual perpetrators and without examining specific

2003), para. 40; Committee on the Rights of the Child, Concluding Observations: Israel, CRC/C/15/Add.195 (9 October 2002), para. 51.

303 Resolution S-2/1, Second session, A/HRC/S-2/1 (11 August 2006), para. 7; Resolution S-9/1, Ninth special session, A/HRC/S-9/2 (16 January 2009), para. 14.

304 Report of the Commission of Inquiry on Lebanon pursuant to Human Rights Council Resolution S-2/1*, A/HRC/3/2 (23 November 2006), paras. 23, 209–212 and 321.

305 Report of the United Nations Fact-Finding Mission on the Gaza Conflict, A/HRC/12/48 (25 September 2009), paras. 1250–1251.

306 Ibid., para. 1733.

requirements, such as the criteria of *mens rea*.[307] For example, a UN Inquiry Commission in North Korea extensively documented the deliberate starvation and deprivation of water of detainees in political prison camps and concluded that these violations amount to torture as a crime against humanity.[308]

The war in Syria has been the object of ten reports by an International Inquiry Commission since 2011. In its September 2015 report, the Commission describes the desperate situation of the Syrian population who are victims of governmental forces, rebels groups and IS. Since 2014, this war has changed from a non-international conflict to an international one with the American-led intervention. The warring parties have made use of siege warfare. The Commission points out that:

> Warring parties encircle densely populated areas, preventing civilians from leaving, and blocking humanitarian access. The besieged communities—thousands of men, women and children—are forced to live under shocking and inhuman conditions. Siege warfare is conducted in a ruthlessly coordinated and planned manner, aimed at forcing a population, collectively, to surrender or suffer starvation. Denial of food, water, electricity and medicine has led to malnutrition and deaths amongst vulnerable groups, such as elderly, infants, young children and persons suffering from chronic illnesses. Trapped without basic necessities and under constant fear of deadly snipers or bombardment, severe psychological trauma and desperation characterize the besieged communities.[309]

In light of these circumstances, the Commission concludes that massive violations of human rights, war crimes and crimes against humanity were committed by the three sides of the conflict: governmental forces, rebel groups and IS. This case illustrates the repercussions of siege warfare on access to water supplies and the violation of the prohibition of starvation, which constitutes a war crime.

IV *Conclusion*

The aim of this section has been to demonstrate that human rights law protects access to water. Together with the resolutions adopted by the UN General Assembly and the Human Rights Council, General Comment No. 15 plays a

---

307 See Evelyne Schmid, *Taking Economic, Social and Cultural Rights Seriously in International Criminal Law* (Cambridge University Press, 2015).

308 North Korea Inquiry Commission, A/HRC/25/CRP.1 (7 February 2014), para. 1053.

309 Report of the Independent International Commission of Inquiry on the Syrian Arab Republic, A/HRC/30/48 (3 September 2015), paras. 99–100.

fundamental role in the definition of the human right to water. Although General Comments are not formally binding, they interpret Covenant rights and contribute to identifying breaches of obligations under the ICESCR. In this context, the ESCR Committee contributes to achieving protection of economic, social and cultural rights. As part of its tasks, the ESCR Committee is authorized to make suggestions and recommendations of a general nature on the basis of its consideration of state reports.[310] Given the interpretative dimension implicit in this task, these 'suggestions' and 'recommendations' may reinforce recognition of the human right to water.

Because the right to water is circumscribed by personal and domestic uses, the scope of this right is restricted to the water essential to the survival of the population during armed conflicts. This definition is based on obligations under IHL. However, the right to water can strengthen IHL by incorporating additional elements into its norms, such as access to water on a non-discriminatory basis and the obligation of states to take measures to prevent third parties from limiting enjoyment of the human right to water.

The right to water imposes obligations, for example, when attacks against water facilities or power plants are carried out by the air forces of a state and impact a population's access to water under its control. Human rights law protects access to water in times of armed conflict by imposing international obligations that must be met by a state vis-à-vis the individuals and communities of living in a territory under its occupation. The right to water strengthens the duties imposed by the rules of international humanitarian law governing occupation. Under a regime of occupation, it may be argued that, in some cases, water resources are exploited beyond the limit set by the rule of usufruct affirmed in Article 55 of the 1907 Hague Regulations. Such overuse imperils the survival of the civilian population, which must be ensured according to the Fourth Geneva Convention and the First Protocol.[311] The lack of respect of the norms of international humanitarian law may lead to multiple violations of the right to water.

D Post-Conflict, Peace-Building and Water

Addressing the human and environmental consequences of armed conflicts requires the commitment of several international actors. The activities of UNEP play a crucial role in this domain. UNEP's activities highlight the need to include environmental protection in the peace-building phase after the

310 Tignino (2016), supra, note 251, p. 244.

311 Article 55 of the Fourth Geneva Convention and Article 69.1 of the First Protocol.

end of armed conflicts. International aid is needed in assessing the damage caused by armed conflicts and in adopting measures to restore the environment. Damage caused to water sources necessitates the adoption by states of surveillance measures to monitor the quality of water resources in order to protect the health of the population and impede long-term damage to water resources. The repair of water networks and power plants also requires significant financial investments by states weakened by a conflict.

The normative framework for the post-conflict phase is not a well-developed field in international law. However, in recent years, there have been encouraging signals like the Resolution on 'Strengthening Legal Protection for Victims of Armed Conflicts' adopted at the 31st Conference of the Red Cross and Red Crescent in 2011. This Resolution advocates for the development of rules and mechanisms dealing with the protection of the environment during and after armed conflicts.[312]

This section will explore the right to humanitarian assistance when access to water is threatened. In so doing, it will pay attention to the role of the ICRC, though its Unit on Water and Habitat (Part I). The chapter will then address the relationship between humanitarian and environmental assistance, highlighting the importance of assessing and monitoring environmental damage (Part II). The field of disarmament law will be studied in order to extrapolate specific rules in the field of environmental protection. Certain agreements dealing with the destruction and removal of weapons contribute to the post-conflict protection of access to water for populations (Part III). Finally, the monograph will examine some legal mechanisms established after armed conflicts that can make important contributions to constructing a long-term peace, thus contributing to peace-building (Part IV).

I *Humanitarian Aid and Communities Affected by Environmental Damage*

Humanitarian aid is required during and after armed conflicts. The sovereign state where the conflict takes place holds primary responsibility for providing food and drinking water to meet the basic survival needs of victims of armed conflicts. When international aid is necessary, priority for its delivery is given to international institutions (intergovernmental and non-governmental organizations) rather than to third states. Humanitarian organizations have the right to offer assistance. In principle, the territorial state must accept this offer when the humanitarian assistance is without discrimination or political

312 International Conference of the Red Cross and Red Crescent, (28 November–1 December 2011), p. 18.

purpose.[313] If the population needs water supplies and the party to a conflict cannot satisfy that need, humanitarian organizations can offer help that must be accepted by the state where the conflict is taking place.[314]

The right to humanitarian assistance is linked to the 'responsibility to protect'.[315] This principle grants a particular importance to the obligation of the state to accept the help offered by third states and humanitarian organizations. The 'collectivisation of the responsibility to protect' imposes obligations on the state where the conflict takes place and on third states. If the basic water needs of a civilian population are threatened by an armed conflict and the party to a conflict is unable to meet those basic needs, the 'responsibility to protect' may be invoked to justify aid from third states and humanitarian organizations.

Humanitarian aid must have certain attributes. It must not discriminate and it must be impartial and neutral. A general definition of these terms is found in the Statutes of the International Red Cross and Red Crescent Movement.[316] The concept of impartiality is defined as follows: "It makes no discrimination as to nationality, race, religious beliefs, class or political opinions. It endeavours

313 In this regard, the International Court of Justice found that: "[T]here can be no doubt that the provision of strictly humanitarian aid to persons or forces in another country, whatever their political affiliations or objectives, cannot be regarded as unlawful intervention, or as in any other way contrary to international law." It adds that: "The characteristics of such aid were indicated in the first and second of the fundamental principles declared by the Twentieth International Conference of the Red Cross, that: 'The Red Cross born of a desire to bring assistance without discrimination to the wounded on the battlefield, endeavours—in its international and national capacity—to prevent and alleviate human suffering wherever it may be found. Its purpose is to protect life and health and to ensure respect for the human being. It promotes mutual understanding, friendship, co-operation and lasting peace amongst all peoples' and that 'It makes no discrimination as to nationality, race, religious beliefs, class or political opinions. It endeavours only to relieve suffering, giving priority to the most urgent cases of distress.'" *Military and Paramilitary Activities in and against Nicaragua (Nicaragua* v. *United States of America), Merits, Judgment, I.C.J. Reports 1986*, p. 14, at para. 242.

314 Nicolai Jorgensen, 'The Protection of Freshwater in Armed Conflict', *Journal of International Law and International Relations*, Vol. 3(2) (2007), pp. 57–96, at p. 80.

315 Laurence Boisson de Chazournes & Luigi Condorelli, 'De la "responsabilité de protéger", ou d'une nouvelle parure pour une notion déjà bien établie', *Revue générale de droit international public*, Vol. 110(1) (2006), pp. 11–18.

316 Statute of the International Red Cross and Red Crescent Movement adopted by the 25th International Conference of the Red Cross at Geneva in 1986, amended in 1995 and 2006, https://www.icrc.org/eng/assets/files/other/statutes-en-a5.pdf, last accessed on 20 January 2016.

to relieve the suffering of individuals, being guided solely by their needs, and to give priority to the most urgent cases of distress."[317] Respect of the principles of non-discrimination, neutrality and impartiality ensure that the entire population has access to humanitarian aid, in particular the supply of food and water to meet basic needs.

Humanitarian personnel must also be protected during and after conflict. Water engineers who repair water pipes and electrical facilities are part of humanitarian personnel and must be respected and protected. Attacks carried out against humanitarian personnel involved "in a humanitarian assistance or peacekeeping mission" are war crimes both in international and non-international armed conflicts.[318] The same protection also covers water engineers working in occupied territories.

The ICRC's crucial role in ensuring access to water during and after armed conflicts was institutionalized through the establishment of the ICRC Water and Habitat Unit in the 1980s. The ICRC not only covers emergency situations but also long-term activities like the restoration of treatment and distribution water networks in urban contexts.[319] Moreover, the ICRC Water and Habitat Unit has brought water to isolated rural areas, as it did, for example, during the Darfur conflict. The measures taken by the ICRC are very important in preventing the spread of water-borne diseases and epidemics. As has been noted, "the objective [of the ICRC Water and Habitat Unit] does not relate to pure engineering. Public health is our primary concern. Access to water is not enough—one must ensure long-term production of a sufficient amount of quality water."[320]

In its efforts to ensure access to water, the ICRC collaborates with other international institutions like UNICEF and the UN High Commissioner for Refugees ('HCR') and with non-governmental organizations like *Médecins sans frontières* ('MSF') and Oxfam. In particular, the HCR ensures the supply of water in refugee camps and works to counter the risk of contamination of water supplies that can endanger the life of refugees and internally displaced people ('IDPs').

---

317 Ibid., p. 5.

318 According to the Statute of the International Criminal Court: "Intentionally directing attacks against personnel, installations, material, units or vehicles involved in a humanitarian assistance or peacekeeping mission in accordance with the Charter of the United Nations, as long as they are entitled to the protection given to civilians or civilian objects under the international law of armed conflict." Articles 8.2 (b) (iii) and 8.2 (e) (iii).

319 Dross et al., supra, note 6.

320 'World Water Day: Restoring Water to Millions of People Affected by Conflict', *International Committee of the Red Cross* (20 March 2007).

II *Humanitarian and Environmental Assistance*

Assistance provided to victims of armed conflicts must continue after a conflict. When hostilities end, people's needs remain pressing and substantial and require international assistance. Environmental threats to the life and health of the population caused by military operations and the use of certain weapons often become visible in the phase following the end of hostilities.

To provide objective and independent assessments of the environmental impacts of military operations, UNEP has established a specific branch to provide post-conflict assessment. In its first study on the impact on the environment of the Kosovo conflict, UNEP emphasized in its report the need to include environment-related activities in humanitarian assistance. The report states:

> [T]here are serious environmental issues, requiring immediate action. The problems identified have important implications for human health and welfare and should therefore be addressed in the *framework of humanitarian assistance* after the conflict.[321]

The environmental impacts of conflict include socio-economic effects on the health and well-being of the population. The measures taken in the environmental field, like restoration of water facilities or monitoring of the quality of water resources, have a humanitarian character.

In contrast to other natural resources, water is the site of a 'natural' link between humanitarian and environmental considerations. For example, in its 2003 Desk Study on Iraq, UNEP noted that:

> The approach of this Desk Study is environmental and technical. The intent is not to attach blame for various environmental problems. Rather, it is to provide an overview of chronic and war-related environmental issues, and to identify the steps needed to safeguard the environment. Top priorities include environmental issues that have a direct link with easing the humanitarian situation, especially the restoration of water, power, sanitation networks and ensuring food security.[322]

Following the Kosovo conflict, UNEP recommended the implementation of rehabilitation projects to address the risks of environmental impact caused by damage to plants located close to water resources. UNEP's recommendation was welcomed by international institutions and donor countries. The Office for the Coordination of Humanitarian Affairs ('OCHA') has included

321 'Kosovo', supra, note 9, p. 31 (italics added by the author).

322 'Desk Study on the Situation of the Environment in Iraq', supra, note 65, p. 6.

humanitarian assistance projects aimed at environmental clean up in its call for proposals. Furthermore, in the 2000 conference organized under the auspices of the Stability Pact for South-Eastern Europe after the Kosovo conflict, environmental clean up projects were included among priority activities for funding. Evaluation of the environmental consequences of the Kosovo conflict is also part of the UN Mission in Kosovo ('UNMIK'), which has an office dedicated to environmental issues.[323]

Humanitarian and environmental assistance is not based on specific international legal instruments. Upon the invitation of states, UNEP will prepare an evaluation analysis on the impact of military operations. However, in one case, the Ministerial Forum of UNEP was the promoter of an environmental study in the Occupied Palestinian territories in 2003. Both parties, Israel and Palestine, agreed to the environmental assessment, opening the way for a field mission by experts from UNEP.[324]

During the conflict in Lebanon in 2006, Israeli attacks against the Jiyeh electrical power plant caused an environmental disaster in the Mediterranean Sea.[325] The sea and air blockade imposed by the Israeli government made monitoring and aerial assessment impossible. In addition, measures to contain and clean up the spill were "unnecessarily obstructed" because of the blockade.[326] Cleaning operations began at the end of the conflict. By then, the oil spill had already polluted much of the Lebanese coast and parts of the Syrian coast. In light of these considerations, the Commission of Inquiry on Lebanon concluded that the government of Israel "should have ordered an immediate relaxation of the blockade to allow the necessary urgent evaluation to be made, assessment measures to be adopted and the necessary clean up measures to be carried out. In the view of the Commission there is no reason that justifies a failure to do so." The Commission also added that: "Israel's engagement in an armed conflict does not exempt it from its general obligation to protect the environment and to react to an environmental catastrophe such as that which took place on the Lebanese coasts."[327]

323 'From Conflict to Sustainable Development. Assessment and Clean-Up in Serbia and Montenegro', *United Nations Environment Program* (2004), p. 9.

324 'Proceedings of the Governing Council at its Twenty-First Session', *United Nations Environment Programme*, GC/21/9 (14 February 2001), p. 5.

325 'Report of the Commission of Inquiry on Lebanon Pursuant to Human Rights Council Resolution S-2/1', A/HRC/3/2 (23 November 2006), paras. 209–220.

326 Ibid., para. 273.

327 Ibid.

The findings of the Commission of Inquiry on Lebanon indicate that the requirement of authorization for environmental aid does not give discretion to a party to a conflict about whether to protect the environment. While there are no specific rules mandating environmental assistance, a party to a conflict should not interfere 'unnecessarily' with such assistance. Environmental assistance cannot be obstructed unless necessary. This restriction shows the importance accorded to environmental protection during and after armed conflicts, while also highlighting the role played by relief agencies in the field of environmental protection.

III *Disarmament Law and the Obligations of Environmental Clean-Up*

Disarmament law contains obligations regarding clean-up that can contribute to the restoration of the environment after an armed conflict. Examples include Protocol II on Prohibitions or Restrictions on the Uses of Mines, Booby-Traps and Other Devices amended on 3 May 1996 to the 1980 Convention on Prohibitions or Restrictions on the Use of Certain Conventional Weapons Which May Be Deemed to Be Excessively Injurious or to Have Indiscriminate Effects ('1996 Protocol II'),[328] and the Convention on the Prohibition of the Development, Production, Stockpiling and Use of Chemical Weapons and on their Destruction of 13 January 1993.

The 1996 Protocol II affirms that states parties to a conflict are responsible for all mines, booby-traps, and other devices employed and have the obligation to undertake to clear, remove and destroy them.[329] Moreover, the Convention on the Prohibition of the Use, Stockpiling, Production and Transfer of Anti-Personnel Mines and on their Destruction of 1997 stipulates that states parties have the duty "to destroy or ensure the destruction of all anti-personnel mines in mined areas under its jurisdiction or control, as soon as possible but not later than ten years after the entry into force of this Convention for that State Party."[330] In addition, the Convention on the Prohibition of the Development, Production, Stockpiling and Use of Chemical Weapons and on their Destruction of 1993 requires states to declare upon accession not only

328 Protocol II on Prohibitions or Restrictions on the Uses of Mines, Booby-Traps and Other Devices as amended on 3 May 1996 to the Convention on Prohibitions or Restrictions on the Use of Certain Conventional Weapons Which May Be Deemed to Be Excessively Injurious or to Have Indiscriminate Effects (3 May 1996).

329 Article 3.2 of the 1996 Protocol II.

330 Article 5.1 of the Convention on the Prohibition of the Use, Stockpiling, Production and Transfer of Anti-Personnel Mines and on their Destruction (18 September 1997).

their stockpiles and production facilities, but also the known or suspected presence of old or abandoned weapons.[331]

Agreements containing obligations about the destruction, removal and clearing of certain types of weapons contribute to the protection of the environment and access to water for local populations after an armed conflict. The Convention on Cluster Munitions of 2008 is one of the first instruments of disarmament law to draw an explicit link between disarmament, the protection of the environment, and the health of populations affected by armed conflict.[332] According to Article 3.2 of this Convention:

> Each State Party undertakes to destroy or ensure the destruction of all cluster munitions referred to in paragraph 1 of this Article as soon as possible but not later than eight years after the entry into force of this Convention for that State Party. Each State Party undertakes to ensure that destruction methods comply with *applicable international standards for protecting public health and the environment.* (Italics added by the author.)

Some instruments of disarmament law also include obligations to take preventive measures. For example, Article 9 of the 2003 Protocol V on Explosive Remnants of War to the 1980 Convention on Prohibitions or Restrictions on the Use of Certain Conventional Weapons Which May Be Deemed to Be Excessively Injurious or to Have Indiscriminate Effects provides that states should "take generic preventive measures aimed at minimising the occurrence of explosive remnants of war."[333] In addition, the 2008 Convention on Cluster Munitions also includes innovative language on victim assistance, affirming that, in accordance with IHL and human rights law, victims should be provided with "age- and gender-sensitive assistance, including medical care, rehabilitation and psychological support, as well as provide for their social and economic inclusion."[334] Disarmament law offers specific justifications for social, economic and environmental assistance after an armed conflict.

---

331 Article 3 of the Convention on the Prohibition of the Development, Production, Stockpiling and Use of Chemical Weapons and on their Destruction (13 January 1993).

332 Article 3.2 of the Convention on Cluster Munitions (30 May 2008).

333 Article 9 of the 2003 Protocol V on Explosive Remnants of War to the 1980 Convention on Prohibitions or Restrictions on the Use of Certain Conventional Weapons Which May Be Deemed to Be Excessively Injurious or to Have Indiscriminate Effects (28 November 2003).

334 Article 5 of the Convention on Cluster Munitions of 2008.

IV *Post-Conflict Legal Avenues to Protect the Human Right to Water*

After an armed conflict, legal mechanisms open to individuals and communities can make important contributions to shaping a long-term peace.[335] In his 2004 report to the Security Council on the rule of law and transitional justice in conflict and post-conflict societies, the Secretary-General underlined the role played by international criminal tribunals and truth commissions in the quest for justice and reconciliation in post-conflict states.[336] The former High Commissioner for Human Rights, Ms. Louise Arbour, has also indicated that mechanisms established after an armed conflict—be it criminal trials, human rights courts or truth commissions—should seek to comprehensively address the root causes of conflicts and promote respect for all human rights.[337]

The judgments of international criminal courts have historically focused on civil and political rights; such judgments rarely address crimes tied to violations of socio-economic rights. However, there are exceptions to this trend. For example, in the *Kupreskic* case, the International Criminal Tribunal for the former Yugoslavia ('ICTY') addressed the issue of whether "economic rights can be considered so fundamental that their denial is capable of constituting [the crime against humanity] of persecution."[338] The Trial Chamber of the ICTY recognized that the comprehensive destruction of homes and property constituted a crime against humanity of persecution when committed with the requisite intent.

The *Kupreskic* judgment illustrates that socio-economic rights can be an underlying element relevant to the crime of persecution. Measures taken against a national group may include a wide spectrum of acts ranging from discriminatory withdrawal of political, social and economic rights to direct physical attacks. Discriminatory practices can also crystallize into a form of attacks against essential means of survival, like water supplies. This point was underlined in the conclusions of the Fact-Finding Mission on the Gaza conflict. The report of the Mission pointed out that:

> The series of acts that deprive Palestinians in the Gaza Strip of their means of sustenance, employment, housing and water [...] could amount

335 Volker Türk, 'Capacity-Building' *in*, Vincent Chetail (ed.), *Post-Conflict Peacebuilding: A Lexicon*, (Oxford University Press, 2009), pp. 34–42.

336 See the UN Secretary-General Report on the Rule of Law and Transitional Justice in Conflict and Post-Conflict Societies, UN Doc. S/2004/616 (23 August 2004).

337 Louise Arbour, 'Economic and Social Justice for Societies in Transition', *Center for Human Rights and Global Justice, New York University Working Paper No. 10* (2006).

338 ICTY, *Kupreskic* et al., Case No. IT-95-16-T, 14 January 2000, para. 630.

> to persecution, a crime against humanity. From the facts available to it, the Mission is of the view that some of the actions of the Government of Israel might justify a competent court finding that crimes against humanity have been committed.[339]

The implication of the Fact-Finding Mission's conclusions is that attacks against water supplies aimed at depriving people of essential means of survival may constitute a crime against humanity.

Human rights mechanisms provide interesting examples of the judicial enforcement of socio-economic rights, including the human right to water, as further discussed in Case Study 15.

The *Social and Economic Rights Action Center and the Center for Economic and Social Rights v. Nigeria* case brought by two NGOs on behalf of the Ogoni people illustrates how the African Commission on Human and Peoples' Rights has dealt with the violations of socio-economic rights. This case concerned attacks perpetrated against the Ogoni people by both the military government of Nigeria and private actors. In finding the Nigerian government in violation of the right to a healthy environment and the right to health, the Commission implicitly considered issues related to the right to water, specifically the contamination of water supplies. The Commission dealt with the contamination and disposal of toxic waste in the Niger Delta area, resulting environmental degradation, and consequent health problems among the Ogoni people.[340] In its decision, the African Commission requested that the government of Nigeria take several measures to ensure protection of the environment and health of the Ogoni people. It appealed to Nigeria "to [undertake] a comprehensive cleanup of lands and rivers damaged by oil operations", "to [ensure] that appropriate environmental and social impact assessments are prepared for any future oil development" and "[to provide] information on health and environmental risks and meaningful access to regulatory and decision-making bodies to communities likely to be affected by oil operations."[341] Despite these appeals, the adverse effects on the environment of oil development activities

339 Fact-Finding Mission on the Conflict in Gaza, Report, UN Doc. A/HRC/12/48 (25 September 2009), para. 75.

340 African Commission on Human and Peoples' Rights, *The Social and Economic Rights Action Center and the Center for Economic and Social Rights v. Nigeria*, Communication No. 155/96, 2001 (27 October 2001), paras. 52–54.

341 Ibid.

in the Delta region and in particular in the Ogoni areas remain issues of concern.[342] In 2006, the government of Nigeria requested UNEP to conduct an environmental assessment of the contamination in the Delta of the Niger River. This analysis was the first study to provide information and technical data on environmental damage.[343]

Case Study 15: The Ogoni case.

In addition, the African Commission on Human and Peoples' Rights rendered an important decision in May 2009 dealing with the right to water and the role that water plays during and after an armed conflict. The Commission decided that the poisoning of water sources during the Darfur conflict amounted to a violation of the African Charter on Human and People's Rights,[344] and it recommended several measures regarding water. In calling for the rehabilitation of economic and social infrastructure in the Darfur provinces, it referred to water services as an element necessary to a dignified and safe return for IDPs and refugees. In calling for the establishment of a National Reconciliation Forum to address the sources of conflict, it targeted the resolution of water rights as a particularly important route to avoiding future conflict.[345]

Several cases concerning armed conflicts have also been addressed through the Inter-American human rights system. In the *Plan de Sanchez* case, the Inter-American Court recommended that the State of Guatemala implement development programmes in the water sector and held that programmes should maintain and improve the sewage system and potable water supplies in the communities affected by the armed conflict.[346] This form of reparation was seen as necessary to implement a social development programme.

342 Concluding Observations of the Committee on the Elimination of Racial Discrimination: Nigeria, UN Doc. CERD/C/NGA/CO/18 (1 November 2005), para. 19.

343 'Natural Resources and Conflict. A Guide for Mediation Practitioners', United Nations Department of Political Affairs and United Nations Environment Programme (2015), p. 31, http://postconflict.unep.ch/publications/UNDPA_UNEP_NRC_Mediation_full.pdf, last accessed on 20 January 2016.

344 African Commission on Human and Peoples' Rights, *Sudan Human Rights Organisation & Centre on Housing Rights and Evictions (COHRE) v. Sudan*, Communication No. 279/03 & 296/05 (27 May 2009), para. 212.

345 Ibid., para. 229 (e) and (f).

346 IACtHR, *Plan de Sánchez Massacre v. Guatemala*, Reparation, Series C No. 116 (19 November 2004), para. 110.

Issues related to access to water also figure in reports adopted by truth commissions. The former High Commissioner for Human Rights has highlighted that truth commissions are particularly well-suited to deal with the investigation and protection of socio-economic rights given that their mandates often include redress for the causes and consequences of a conflict.[347] For example, in the final report of the Timor-Leste Commission for Reception, Truth and Reconciliation, the Commission dedicates an entire chapter to the impacts of the Indonesian occupation on the socio-economic rights of the people of Timor-Leste.[348]

Some truth commissions have recommended that states should adopt certain social policies at the end of an armed conflict. For example, in the reparation programme it recommended to the government, the Sierra Leone Truth and Reconciliation Commission dealt with several socio-economic rights like health and education. It noted that social services such as health "should be universally provided," particularly to vulnerable people whose needs require prioritization.[349] Furthermore, the report "emphasizes the recommendation to bring [...] service delivery to people throughout Sierra Leone. The government must be seen to be establishing infrastructure and delivering health, education [...]."[350] Those recommendations towards achieving national reconciliation may be interpreted as including access to water facilities. Another example is provided by the Moroccan Equity and Reconciliation Commission, established to inquire into human rights violations occurring between 1956 and 1999.[351] The Commission recommended communal reparations to strengthen the economic and social development of specific regions that

347 Arbour, supra, note 337. See also 'Rule of Law Tools for Post-Conflict States. Truth Commissions' (United Nations, 2006).

348 In its report the Commission noted that "the impact of the [socio-economic] conditions in which [the population] lived, while often less remarked on, was equally damaging and possibly more long-lasting" than the threats to civil and political rights. Timor-Leste Commission for Reception, Truth and Reconciliation, *Chega!* (October 2005), para. 1. The Commission found that Indonesia failed to "meet the basic needs of the population for food, shelter and essential medicines" and caused "their economic and social situations to deteriorate". Ibid., para. 131.

349 Sierra Leone Truth and Reconciliation Commission, *Witness to Truth*, Vol. 2 (2004), p. 235, para. 32.

350 Ibid., p. 123, para. 41.

351 The most serious violations of human rights took place in the aftermath of the attempted military coups and during the armed conflict with the Polisario Front within the context of the Western Sahara conflict. See Amnesty International, *Broken Promises: The Equity and Reconciliation Commission and its Follow-Up* (2008).

were particularly affected by political violence and were marginalized and excluded.[352] Economic and social development must include access to safe drinking water supplies and basic sanitation services.

V *Conclusion*

Post-conflict situations and peace-building raise various issues, including environmental assistance, the obligations of clean-up, and the 'responsibility to protect' the population from a deliberated limitation to those water supplies essential to the survival of the civilian population. In these situations, the ICRC plays a crucial role in ensuring supplies of drinking water to the population. This role was strengthened with the establishment of the ICRC Water and Habitat Unit in the 1980s. The actions of the ICRC cover situations of emergency and long-term activities. Disarmament law also defines specific obligations to address environmental assistance after an armed conflict. A significant example is the Convention on Cluster Munitions of 2008 and its explicit link between the protection of the environment and the health of the population during and after an armed conflict. Legal mechanisms under international criminal law and human rights law provide avenues to address violations of IHL and human rights law. Criminal trials, human rights tribunals and truth commissions are among the many means by which peace can be pursued after an armed conflict. Restoring the rule of law at the end of a conflict is a thorny question. There is no silver bullet that restores the rule of law and ensures a lasting peace. Approaches must be adapted to the specificities of the conflict and the needs of the affected communities.[353] Each of these mechanisms has potential ramifications on access to water and the protection of water resources.

Perspectives: A Specific Instrument Dedicated to the Protection of Water During and After Armed Conflicts?

There is a pressing need to strengthen the protection of water resources and installations during and after armed conflicts. The post-conflict environmental assessment reports prepared by UNEP establish the magnitude of the impact of conflicts on water resources. In May 1999, while the Kosovo war

352 The Moroccan Equity and Reconciliation Commission, Three Part Summary of the Final Report (2005), p. 5.

353 Jane E. Stromseth, 'Rule of Law Symposium Strengthening Demand for the Rule of Law in Post-Conflict Societies', *Minnesota Journal of International Law*, Vol. 18 (2009), pp. 415–424.

was raging, the Director of UNEP created a Special Balkans Team tasked with assessing the conflict's environmental impact. This first post-conflict environmental assessment led to the creation in 2001 of a permanent institutional mechanism, the UNEP Post-Conflict Branch. The Post-Conflict Branch has drafted approximately forty environmental assessment reports in the wake of armed conflicts and natural disasters. As an example, UNEP reported that, during the 2006 Lebanon conflict, the Israeli army's attack against the oil reserves near the Jiyeh electrical power plant caused thousands of tons of oil to spill into the Mediterranean Sea, affecting its living marine resources, the coastline of neighbouring countries such as Syria, and groundwater in Lebanon.[354] With regard to the Kosovo conflict, UNEP's environmental assessment report emphasized that the bombing of industrial installations in Pancevo and Novi Sad in the Former Republic of Yugoslavia had "seriously polluted certain sites" and that a long-term monitoring programme was required to reduce pollution.[355] International practice demonstrates a need to expand the obligation to protect water resources in times of armed conflict. In order to prevent long-term environmental damage, this obligation should not be limited to a prohibition on causing widespread, long-lasting and serious damage, but should include causing damage below this threshold.

We have already evoked the principle of systemic integration, based on Article 31 (3) (c) of the Vienna Convention on the Law of Treaties. This principle ensures that norms of IHL must be interpreted in light of the relevant rules and principles of international law applicable to the relations between the parties. This principle provides a method of interpretation to ensure that specialized laws are applied and interpreted in a manner consistent with general international law.[356] International humanitarian rules are "part of international law and must be interpreted against the general background of its rules and principles."[357] The principle of systemic integration ensures that other international legal rules are taken into account in the interpretation of international humanitarian instruments. International courts, including

354 'Lebanon', supra, note 65, pp. 6 and 48.

355 'Kosovo', supra, note 9, p. 76.

356 'Fragmentation of international law: Difficulties arising from the diversification and expansion of international law', Study Group of the International Law Commission, A/CN.4/L.682 (2006), para. 414.

357 Hersch Lauterpacht, 'Restrictive Interpretation and the Principle of Effectiveness in the Interpretation of Treaties', *British Yearbook of International Law*, Vol. 26 (1949), pp. 48–85, at p. 76.

the International Court of Justice, have promoted an evolving interpretation of legal instruments.[358]

The protection of water resources in times of armed conflict must evolve while taking into account the panoply of existing international norms. These norms spring from different normative sources. In order to protect water resources and ensure that the population has access to vital resources such as water, the law applicable to armed conflicts must be understood in a context broader than IHL. Such a reading of the law would mitigate the impact of armed conflicts on water resources and establish the conditions required to promote peace-building after armed conflicts.[359]

The fragmentation of international law on the protection of water during and after armed conflicts has hampered the development of effective instruments and policies to minimize, assess, and address wartime damage. International law does not have a specific instrument solely devoted to the protection of water in times of armed conflict. However, the 1954 Convention for the Protection of Cultural Property in the Event of Armed Conflict is an example of an international agreement that is devoted to the protection of a specific civilian object, i.e. cultural property.[360] The adoption of a treaty dedicated only to water would bring the advantage of gathering all the applicable provisions in a single instrument. Such an instrument would assemble rules from different areas of international law and would therefore broaden the scope of the law applicable to the protection of water during and after armed conflicts.

A new legal instrument devoted to the protection of water during and after armed conflicts should give particular weight to the protection of areas of major ecological and human importance for access to water, like transboundary aquifers and international watercourses. A proposal to provide special protection to areas of major ecological importance was made during the drafting of the 1977 Protocols to the Geneva Conventions, when a working group submitted a proposal that "publicly recognized nature reserves with adequate

358 See PCA, *Belgium/Netherlands ("Iron Rhine Arbitration")*, Award of 24 May 2005, para. 58. ICJ, *Legal Consequences for States of the Continued Presence of South Africa in Namibia (South West Africa) notwithstanding Security Council Resolution 276 (1970), Advisory Opinion, I.C.J. Reports 1971*, p. 16, at para. 53; *Gabčíkovo-Nagymaros Project (Hungary/Slovakia), Judgment, I.C.J. Reports 1997*, p. 7, at para. 112.

359 Tignino (2011), supra, note 4, pp. 434–440.

360 See the Convention for the Protection of Cultural Property in the Event of Armed Conflict (14 May 1954). The list of the World Heritage Convention already includes water resource sites such the Lakes of Ounianga in Chad and the Lower Valley of the Omo River in Ethiopia.

markings and boundaries declared as such to the adversary shall be protected and respected except when such reserves are used specifically for military purposes."[361] The proposal was not adopted, however.[362]

This proposal for codification of legal norms about water in a single instrument should be compared to the system of specially protected areas for cultural property. The Second Protocol to the Convention for the Protection of Cultural Property in the Event of Armed Conflict establishes a system of enhanced protection, under which cultural property of special significance for humanity is entered on a list and the parties to the Protocol undertake never to use it to support military operations.[363] A system of listed sites also exists under the World Heritage Convention.[364] This Convention requires states "not to take any deliberate measures which might damage directly or indirectly the cultural and natural heritage."[365] It also provides for the inscription on the List of World Heritage in Danger of any site endangered by "the outbreak or the threat of an armed conflict."[366] As of October 2016, 55 sites are included in the List of World Heritage in Danger. Many of them are located in areas of armed conflict, like Afghanistan, Iraq and Syria. The Second Protocol to the Convention for the Protection of Cultural Property in the Event of Armed Conflict and the World Heritage Convention could inspire the creation of special areas related to water resources that are significant for providing drinking water and for the protection of the environment. These areas would be demilitarized and especially protected by international law.

The legal development of a specific instrument on water may be linked to current reform efforts in the field of IHL. In 2011, the 31st Conference of the Red Cross and Red Crescent proposed the creation of a mechanism to monitor the environmental damage caused by violations of IHL in international and non-international armed conflicts.[367] The aim of this mechanism would be to

361 Sandoz; Swinarski & Zimmerman, supra, note 7, p. 663.

362 'Second Report on the Protection of the Environment in Relation to Armed Conflicts submitted by Marie Jacobsson', International Law Commission, A/CN.4/685 (28 May 2015), p. 69.

363 Second Protocol to the Convention for the Protection of Cultural Property in the Event of Armed Conflict (1999).

364 On the relationship between water and the World Heritage Convention, see Boisson de Chazournes, supra, note 177, pp. 132–133.

365 Article 6.3 of the Convention concerning the Protection of the World Cultural and Natural Heritage (World Heritage Convention) (16 November 1972).

366 Article 11.4.

367 It should be noted that the ICRC and the government of Switzerland are supporting the initiative to create a mechanism to strengthen compliance with international humanitarian

monitor the environmental damage, investigate the violations of international rules and decide on appropriate forms of reparation.[368] These reparations could include, for example, the decontamination of water resources that may affect the health of the population in the short- and long-term. This proposal is particularly ground-breaking as it points out that such mechanisms should assess environmental damage caused by both lawful and unlawful military operations. Significant harm to water resources may result from the destruction of power plants, chemical and industrial sites or other attacks against military objectives. This mechanism is a promising avenue to increasing the protection of water resources. The UNEA Resolution adopted in 2016 could also be used as an entry point for developing a specific instrument dedicated to the protection of water during and after armed conflicts.[369]

New norms on increasing environmental assistance should also be developed, building on the examples of the obligations contained in instruments of disarmament law like the Convention on the Prohibition of the Use, Stockpiling, Production and Transfer of Anti-personnel Mines and on their Destruction of 1997 and the 2003 Protocol V on Explosive Remnants of War to the 1980 Conventional Weapons Convention.[370]

The recommendations to create new rules and mechanisms to monitor environmental damage to water resources and find appropriate forms of rehabilitation of the environment at the end of conflict play an important role in thinking about the development of international legal norms protecting water resources during and after armed conflicts. Monitoring mechanisms should complement the norms on the protection of water resources and the practice of using them may contribute to defining the contours of these norms. These mechanisms help to apply and interpret principles and rules applicable during and after armed conflicts. These legal developments may be supported by the work of UNEP and other actors involved in the assessment and collection of data on the environmental impacts of armed conflicts. New rules and

law. States are nevertheless reluctant to agree to this proposal. See 'No agreement by States on mechanism to strengthen compliance with rules of war', International Committee of the Red Cross, Press Release, 10 December 2015.

368 'Strengthening Legal Protection for the Victims of Armed Conflicts', 31th International Conference of the Red Cross and Red Crescent (28 November–1 December 2011), p. 18.

369 United Nations Environment Assembly (UNEA) Resolution, UNEP/EA.2/ L.16/REV.1 (May 2016).

370 See also the recommendations on increasing the environmental protection during and after an armed conflict made by the non-governmental organization, Toxic Remnants of War. 'Environmental Mechanics: Re-Imaging Post-Conflict Environmental Assistance', *Toxic Remnants of War* (2015).

mechanisms on the assessment and monitoring of environmental damage are essential to improve the protection of water resources and water installations during and after armed conflicts.

Bibliography

Alam, Undala, 'India and Pakistan's Truculent Cooperation: Can it Continue?', *in*, Laurence Boisson de Chazournes; Christina Leb & Mara Tignino (eds.), *International Law and Freshwater: the Multiple Challenges* (Edward Elgar, 2013), pp. 406–420.

Arbour, Louise, 'Economic and Social Justice for Societies in Transition', *Center for Human Rights and Global Justice, New York University—Law Working Paper No. 10* (2006).

Boisson de Chazournes, Laurence & Condorelli, Luigi, 'De la "responsabilité de protéger", ou d'une nouvelle parure pour une notion déjà bien établie', *Revue générale de droit international public*, Vol. 110(1) (2006), pp. 11–18.

Boisson de Chazournes, Laurence, *Fresh Water in International Law* (Oxford University Press, 2013).

Bothe, Michael et al., 'International Law Protecting the Environment during Armed Conflict: Gaps and Opportunities', *International Review of the Red Cross*, Vol. 92 (879), (2010), pp. 569–592.

Bothe, Michael, 'Customary International Humanitarian Law: Some Reflections on the ICRC Study', *Yearbook of International Humanitarian Law*, Vol. 8 (2007), pp. 143–178.

Bothe, Michael, 'The Protection of the Environment in Times of Armed Conflict: Legal Rules, Uncertainty, Deficiencies and Possible Developments', *German Yearbook of International Law*, Vol. 34 (1992), pp. 54–62.

Bothe, Michael; Partsch, Karl J. & Solf, Waldemar A., *New Rules for Victims of Armed Conflicts: Commentary on the Two Protocols Additional to the Geneva Conventions of 1949* (Martinus Nijhoff Publishers, 1982).

Boutruche, Theo, 'Le statut de l'eau en droit international humanitaire', *International Review of the Red Cross*, Vol. 82 (840) (2000), pp. 887–916.

Bouvier, Antoine, 'Protection of the Natural Environment in Time of Armed Conflict', *International Review of the Red Cross*, No. 272 (1992), pp. 438–458.

Browder, Greg & Ortolano, Leonard, 'The Evolution of an International Water Resources Management Regime in the Mekong River Basin', *Natural Resources Journal*, Vol. 40 (2000), pp. 499–531.

Bruch, Carl, 'All's not Fair in (Civil) War: Criminal Liability of Environmental Damage in Internal Armed Conflict', *Vermont Law Review*, Vol. 25(3) (2000–2001), pp. 695–752.

Caflisch, Lucius, 'La Convention du 21 mai 1997 sur l'utilisation des cours d'eau à des fins autres que la navigation', *Annuaire français de droit international*, Vol. 43(1) (1997), pp. 751–798.

Cassese, Antonio, 'The Martens Clause: Half a Loaf or Simply Pie in the Sky?', *European Journal of International Law*, Vol. 11(1) (2000), pp. 187–216.

Cazala, Julien, 'Le droit international de l'eau et les différends relatifs au Tigre et à l'Euphrate', *in*, Laurence Boisson de Chazournes & Salman M.A. Salman (eds.), *Water Resources and International Law*, The Hague Academy of International Law (Brill, 2004), pp. 533–575.

Coomans, Fons, 'Some Remarks on the Extraterritorial Application of the International Covenant on Economic, Social and Cultural Rights', *in*, Fons Coomans & Menno Kamminga (eds.), *Extraterritorial Application of Human Rights Treaties* (Intersentia, 2004), pp. 183–200.

Costa, Pascale, 'Les effets de la guerre sur les traités relatifs au Danube, dans le cadre d'une étude globale du droit conventionnel du Danube', *in*, Ralph Zacklin & Lucius Caflisch (eds.), *The Legal Regime of International Rivers and Lakes* (Martinus Nijhoff, 1981), pp. 203–245.

Desgagne, Richard, 'The Prevention of Environmental Damage in Time of Armed Conflict: Proportionality and Precautionary Measures', *Yearbook of International Humanitarian Law*, Vol. 3 (2000) pp. 109–129.

Di Stefano, Giovanni & Henry, Etienne, 'Final Provisions, including the Martens Clause', *in*, Andrew Clapham; Paola Gaeta & Marco Sassòli (eds.), *The 1949 Geneva Conventions. A Commentary* (Oxford University Press, 2015), pp. 155–190.

Droege, Cordula & Tougas, Marie-Louise, 'The Protection of the Natural Environment in Armed Conflict—Existing Rules and Need for Further Legal Protection', *Nordic Journal of International Law*, Vol. 82 (2013), pp. 21–52.

Droege, Cordula, 'Elective Affinities? Human Rights and Humanitarian Law', *International Review of the Red Cross*, Vol. 90 (871) (2008), pp. 501–548.

Droege, Cordula, 'The Interplay Between International Humanitarian Law and International Human Rights Law in Situations of Armed Conflict', *Israel Law Review*, Vol. 40(2) (2007), pp. 310–355.

Dross, Jean-Philippe et al., 'Urban Services during protracted armed conflict', *International Committee of the Red Cross* (2015).

Dörmann, Knut, 'Preparatory Commission for the International Criminal Court: The Elements of War Crimes', *International Review of the Red Cross*, Vol. 83 (842) (2001), pp. 461–487.

Fitzmaurice, Gerald, 'The Juridical Clauses of Peace Treaties', *in*, *Collected Courses of the Hague Academy of International Law*, Vol. 73 (1948), pp. 255–367.

Ford, Jolion, 'Engaging the Private Sector in Post-Conflict Recovery', Paper No. 269, *Institute for Security Studies* (2014).

Gleick, Peter, 'Water, Drought, Climate Change, and Conflict in Syria', *Weather, Climate and Society*, Vol. 6(3) (2014), pp. 331–340.

Greenwood, Christopher, 'Historical Development and Legal Basis', *in*, Dieter Fleck (ed.), *The Handbook of International Humanitarian Law* (Oxford University Press, 2008), pp. 1–43.

Henckaerts, Jean-Marie & Doswald-Beck, Louise (eds.), *Customary International Humanitarian Law, Vol. 1: Rules* (Cambridge University Press, 2005).

Hulme, Karen, 'Taking Care to Protect the Environment against Damage: a Meaningless Obligation?', *International Review of the Red Cross*, Vol. 92 (879) (2010), pp. 675–691.

International Law and Policy Institute, 'Protection of the Natural Environment in Armed Conflict. An Empirical Study', Report 12 (2014).

Jorgensen, Nikolai, 'The Protection of Freshwater in Armed Conflict', *Journal of International Law and International Relations*, Vol. 3(2) (2007), pp. 57–96.

Kiss, Alexander, 'Les Protocoles additionnels aux Conventions de Genève de 1949 et la protection des biens de l'environnement', *in*, *Études et essais sur le droit international humanitaire et sur les principes de la Croix-Rouge en l'honneur de Jean Pictet* (International Committee of the Red Cross, 1984), pp. 229–262.

Kraska, James, 'Sustainable Development is Security: The Role of Transboundary River Agreements as a Confidence Building Measure (CBM) in South Asia', *Yale Journal of International Law*, Vol. 28 (2003), pp. 465–503.

Künnemann, Rolf, 'Extraterritorial Application of the International Covenant on Economic, Social and Cultural Rights', *in*, Fons Coomans & Menno Kamminga (eds.), *Extraterritorial Application of Human Rights Treaties* (Intersentia, 2004), pp. 201–232.

Lacroze, Luc, *L'aménagement du Mékong (1957–1997). L'échec d'une grande ambition?* (L'Harmattan, 1998).

Lauterpacht, Hersch, 'Restrictive Interpretation and the Principle of Effectiveness in the Interpretation of Treaties', *British Yearbook of International Law*, Vol. 26 (1949), pp. 48–85.

Leb, Christina, 'The Right to Water in a Transboundary Context: Seminal Trends', *Water International*, Vol. 37(2) (2012), pp. 640–653.

Levie, Howard, *The Code of International Armed Conflict*, Vol. 2 (Oceana Publications, 1986).

Von Lossow, Tobias, 'Water as Weapon: IS on the Euphrates and Tigris. The Systematic Instrumentalisation of Water Entails Conflicting IS Objectives', *German Institute for International and Security Studies* (2016).

Manner, Eero, & Metsälampi, Veli-Martti, *The Work of the International Law Association on the Law of International Water Resources* (Helsinki: International Law Association, 1998).

McCaffrey, Stephen, *The Law of International Watercourses* (2nd edition, Oxford University Press, 2007).

McNair, Arnold D., 'Les effets de la guerre sur les traités', *in*, *Collected Courses of the Hague Academy of International Law*, Vol. 49 (Brill, 1937), pp. 523–586.

Meron, Theodor, 'The Martens Clause, Principles of Humanity and Dictates of Public Conscience', *American Journal of International Law*, Vol. 94 (2000), pp. 78–89.

Mollard-Bannelier, Karine, *La protection de l'environnement en temps de conflit armé* (Pedone, 2001).

Momtaz, Djamchid, 'Le recours à l'arme nucléaire et la protection de l'environnement: l'apport de la Cour internationale de Justice', *in*, Laurence Boisson de Chazournes & Philippe Sands (eds.), *International Law, the International Court of Justice and Nuclear Weapons* (Cambridge University Press, 1999), pp. 354–374.

Pictet, Jean, *Development and Principles of International Humanitarian Law. Course given in July 1982 at the University of Strasbourg as part of the courses organized by the International Institute of Human Rights* (Martinus Nijhoff Publishers, 1982).

Remans, Wilfried, 'Water and War', *Humantäres Völkerrecht*, Vol. 8(1) (1995), pp. 1–14.

Richard, Vanessa, *La coopération sur la gestion des cours d'eau internationaux en Asie* (La Documentation française, 2005).

Rieu-Clarke, Alistair; Moynihan, Ruby & Magsig, Bjørn-Oliver, *UN Watercourses Convention. User's Guide* (Center for Water Law, Policy and Science, University of Dundee, 2012).

Salman, M.A. Salman & Uprety, Kishor, *Conflict and Cooperation on South Asia's International Rivers. A Legal Perspective* (World Bank, 2003).

Salman, M.A. Salman & McInerney-Lankford, S., *The Human Right to Water: Legal and Policy Dimensions* (World Bank, 2004).

Salman, M.A. Salman, 'The Mediation of International Water Disputes—The Indus, the Jordan and the Nile Basins Interventions', *in*, Laurence Boisson de Chazournes. Christina Leb & Mara Tignino (eds.), *International Law and Freshwater. The Multiple Challenges* (Edward Elgar, 2013), pp. 360–405.

Sandoz, Yves; Swinarski, Christophe & Zimmerman, Bruno, 'Commentary on the Additional Protocols of 8 June 1977 to the Geneva Conventions of 12 August 1949', *International Committee of the Red Cross* (Martinus Nijhoff, 1987).

Sassòli, Marco, 'Le droit international humanitaire, une lex specialis par rapport aux droits humains?', *in*, Andreas Auer; Alexander Fluckiger & Michel Hottelier (eds.), *Les droits de l'homme et la Constitution: études en l'honneur du Professeur Giorgio Malinverni* (Schuttless, 2007), pp. 375–395.

Schmid, Evelyne, *Taking Economic, Social and Cultural Rights Seriously in International Criminal Law* (Cambridge University Press, 2015).

Schwarzenberger, George, *The Legality of Nuclear Weapons* (Stevens and Sons, 1958).

Shelton, Dinah, 'Human Rights and the Environment: Substantive Rights', *in*, Malgosia Fitzmaurice; David M. Ong & Panos Merkouris (eds.), *Research Handbook on International Environmental Law* (Edward Elgar, 2011), pp. 265–283.

Singh, Nagendra & MacWhinney, Edward, *Nuclear Weapons and Contemporary International Law* (2nd ed., Martinus Nijhoff Publishers, 1989).

Sjöstedt, Britta, 'The Role of Multilateral Environmental Agreements in Armed Conflict: "Green-keeping" in Virunga Park. Applying the UNESCO World Heritage Convention in the Armed Conflict of the Democratic Republic of Congo', *Nordic Journal of International Law*, Vol. 82 (2013), pp. 129–153.

Stromseth, Jane, 'Rule of Law Symposium Strengthening Demand for the Rule of Law in Post-Conflict Societies', *Minnesota Journal of International Law*, Vol. 18 (2009), pp. 415–424.

Stucki, Philipp, 'Water Wars or Water Peace? Rethinking the Nexus between Water Scarcity and Armed Conflict', Occasional Paper No. 3, *Programme for Strategic and International Security Studies* (2005).

Tanzi, Attila, 'Reducing the Gap between International Water Law and Human Rights Law: The UNECE Protocol on Water and Health', *Review of European, Comparative & International Environmental Law* (*RECIEL*), Vol. 12(3) (2010), pp. 267–285.

Ticehurst, Rupert, 'The Martens Clause and the Laws of Armed Conflict', *International Review of the Red Cross*, No. 824 (1997), pp. 133–142.

Tignino, Mara, *L'eau et la guerre: éléments pour un régime juridique*, Geneva Academy of International Humanitarian Law and Human Rights Law (Bruylant, 2011).

Tignino, Mara, 'L'incidence des conflits armés sur le régime des fleuves internationaux', *in*, Bogdan Aurescu & Alain Pellet (eds.), *L'actualité du droit des fleuves internationaux* (Pedone, 2010), pp. 187–201.

Tignino, Mara, 'Principle 23: The Environment of Oppressed People', *in*, Jorge E. Viñuales (ed.), *The Rio Declaration on Environment and Development* (Oxford University Press, 2015), pp. 557–568.

Tignino, Mara, 'Quasi-Judicial Bodies', *in*, Catherine Bröllman & Yannick Radi (eds.), *Research Handbook on the Theory and Practice of International Law-Making* (Edward Elgar, 2016), pp. 242–260.

Tignino, Mara, 'The Legal Regime of Natural Resources in Times of Armed Conflict and its Weaknesses', *in*, Yann Kerbrat & Sandrine Maljean-Dubois (eds.), *The Transformation of International Environmental Law* (Hart & Pedone, 2011) pp. 193–207.

Tignino, Mara, 'The Right to Water and Sanitation in Post-Conflict Peacebuiding, *Water International*, No. 2 (2011), pp. 241–248.

Tougas, Marie-Louise, 'Principle 24: The Environment in Armed Conflict', *in*, Jorge E. Viñuales (ed.), *The Rio Declaration on Environment and Development* (Oxford University Press, 2015), pp. 569–584.

Türk, Volker, 'Capacity-Building', *in*, Vincent Chetail (ed.), *Post-Conflict Peacebuilding: A Lexicon* (Oxford University Press, 2009), pp. 34–42.

Vöneky, Silja, 'A New Shield for the Environment: Peacetime Treaties as Legal Restraints of Wartime Damage', *Review of European Community & International Environmental Law*, Vol. 9(1) (2000), pp. 20–32.

Zemmali, Ameur, 'La protection de l'eau en période de conflit armé', *International Review of the Red Cross*, Vol. 77 (815) (1995), pp. 601–615.

www.ingramcontent.com/pod-product-compliance
Lightning Source LLC
Chambersburg PA
CBHW071353230926
1846CB00002B/532